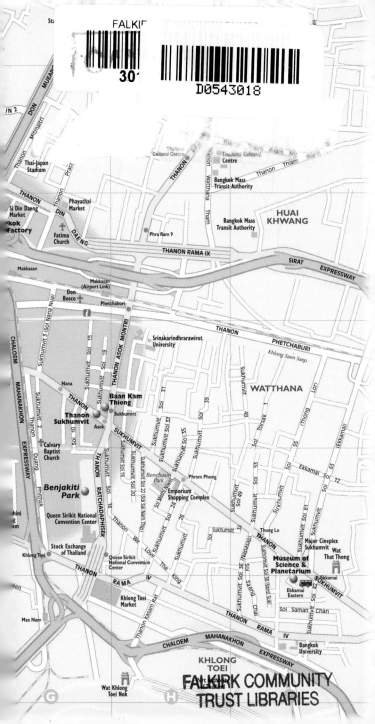

CITYPACK GUIDE TO
Bangkok

How to Use
This Book

KEY TO SYMBOLS

✚ Map reference to the accompanying fold-out map

✉ Address

☎ Telephone number

🕓 Opening/closing times

🍴 Restaurant or café

🚇 Nearest rail station

Ⓜ Nearest Metro (subway) station

🚌 Nearest bus route

⛴ Nearest riverboat or ferry stop

♿ Facilities for visitors with disabilities

❓ Other practical information

▷ Further information

ℹ Tourist information

✋ Admission charges: Expensive (over 200B), Moderate (100B–200B) and Inexpensive (less than 100B)

This guide is divided into four sections

• Essential Bangkok: An introduction to the city and tips on making the most of your stay.
• Bangkok by Area: We've broken the city into four areas, and recommended the best sights, shops, entertainment venues, nightlife and restaurants. Suggested walks help you to explore on foot. Farther Afield takes you out of the city.
• Where to Stay: The best hotels, whether you're looking for luxury, budget or something in between.
• Need to Know: The info you need to make your trip run smoothly, including getting about by public transportation, weather tips, emergency phone numbers and useful websites.

Navigation In the Bangkok by Area chapter, we've given each area its own color, which is also used on the locator maps throughout the book and the map on the inside front cover.

Maps The fold-out map accompanying this book is a comprehensive street plan of Bangkok. The grid on this fold-out map is the same as the grid on the locator maps within the book. We've given grid references within the book for each sight and listing.

Contents

Introducing Bangkok

The energy of Bangkok is intoxicating and visitors, whether they stay just a couple of days to see the main sights or spend longer and look a little deeper, come away with lasting impressions of a city that lives life in the fast lane.

The view from the road or train into the city is of futuristic high rises and multilane highways, but at street level the contrasts are stark. The many street markets buzz with activity as residents bargain hard for food and necessities, but nearby well-heeled shoppers head into glitzy shopping malls packed with designer brands. In the early morning the monks, eyes down and clutching their traditional bowls, walk silently in line along the streets collecting alms from the locals; just behind them bleary-eyed bar girls and revelers make their way home.

The evening crowds meander along the narrow streets taking their time in choosing what to eat from one of the many street foodstands, where the food is freshly cooked; nearby the choice of restaurants is legendary, ranging from places selling simple traditional dishes to those with white tablecloths, gleaming cutlery and rooftops with views to die for.

The end of the 20th century saw an extraordinary building boom here—with a subsequent increase in traffic. The Skytrain and Metro system relieve the pressure and these transportation lines continue to be extended, opening up new parts of the city to be explored. The constant movement of boats on the Chao Phraya River is relentless, but a river boat is still a fun and efficient way of getting around, particularly in the Rattanakosin area.

Since 2006 Thailand has seen turbulent political times, most played out in Bangkok, but the impact on visitors has been minimal. In fact, in 2013 Bangkok was the world's most visited city, with 16 million international arrivals. Wherever you go and whatever you do, join in the all-pervasive *sanuk* (fun) and any language barriers will melt away.

FACTS AND FIGURES

- 8.5 million residents
- 95 percent of Bangkokians are Buddhists
- Bangkok's full ceremonial name runs to 169 characters—Krung Thep Mahanakhon Amon Rattanakosin Mahinthara Ayuthaya Mahadilok Phop Noppharat Ratchathani Burirom Udomratchaniwet Mahasathan Amon Piman Awatan Sathit Sakkathattiya Witsanukam Prasit.

SABAI SABAI

For Thais, happiness is closely linked to tranquility and while the word *sabai* is often translated as "happy," its true meaning is closer to "relaxed" or "comfortable." It's a sense of wellness. One way Thais emphasize an adjective is to simply repeat it. Think of "not a care in the world" and you have a fairly accurate English translation of *sabai sabai*.

LONG LIVE THE KING

The national anthem is played at Hualamphong Station, before movies and on television at 8am and 6pm daily. HM King Bhumibol Adulyadej (Rama IX), the world's longest reigning monarch, is adored in a way that is unfamiliar to many foreigners. The king has also earned wide esteem for his public projects and able leadership.

THE NEW CAPITAL

In 1768, after the Burmese destroyed Ayutthaya, General Phraya Taksin established a new capital at Thonburi, where he was crowned King Boromaraja IV (known as King Taksin). In 1782, Taksin was deposed by a general, who became Rama I. His new capital was Krung Threp (City of Angels); today the city is known as Bangkok.

5

A Short Stay in Bangkok

DAY 1

Morning Start early, before it gets steamy, with a visit to **Wat Phra Kaeo** (▷ 36) and the **Grand Palace** (▷ 24–25), two superb examples of Thai art and architecture, which cannot be missed. Stroll over to the temple compound of **Wat Pho** (▷ 34–35), to admire the huge reclining Buddha, the carvings of the *Ramakien,* and then finish off the visit with an authentic Thai massage on the grounds.

Lunch There are few lunch options in this area, so walk across the green oasis of **Sanam Luang** (▷ 30) and then hop on a ferry from Tha Tien pier to Tha Phra Athit for some tasty vegetarian food at **May Kaidee's** (▷ 48).

Afternoon After lunch walk around Banglamphu and Thanon Khao San and shop for some inexpensive souvenirs.

Mid-afternoon Around 3pm arrange a long-tail boat to take you from Tha Phra Athit pier—to the river canals in Thonburi—to perhaps **Khlong Bangkok Yai** (▷ 100–101), with a stop at the dazzling Temple of the Dawn, **Wat Arun** (▷ 32).

Dinner Go for cocktails on the immensely high roof terrace of **Vertigo** (▷ 68), and then take a taxi to **Eat Me** (▷ 66) for some delightful fusion food and great atmosphere.

Evening After a long day, walk to Silom Road and check out the many and diverse goods stalls at the night market around **Thanon Patpong** (▷ 56).

DAY 2

Morning Have a leisurely breakfast on the beautiful terrace of the **Mandarin Oriental Hotel** (▷ 58, 112), watching the busy traffic on the Chao Phraya River. Stroll over to the delightful **Museum for Bangkokians** (▷ 58) with its peaceful garden and interesting mix of Thai, Chinese, Indian and European elements (call ahead for a guided tour by the lady who grew up there). For a very different and definitely more glamorous approach to Thai architecture, take a taxi, or Skytrain, to **Baan Jim Thompson** (▷ 74) near Siam Square, with one of the world's best collections of traditional Thai paintings.

Lunch After a visit to the elegant and fascinating house on the *khlong*, have lunch at the stylish bar and restaurant in Jim Thompson's House.

Afternoon It is a short walk from the house to Siam Square, where you can spend the afternoon shopping at the **Siam Paragon** shopping mall (▷ 86), **Narai Phand** emporium (▷ 87) and **Emporium** (▷ 86). If you prefer more architecture to shopping, head for the Dusit area and visit the stunning royal **Phra Thi Nang Vimanmek** (▷ 77) or take a guided cycling tour (▷ 119) and explore beyond the main drag. Relax before dinner with a good massage at one of the city's many spas (▷ 46, 65, 91); **Ruen-Nuad** (▷ 65) is particularly recommended.

Dinner Head for one of the trendy eateries off Sukhumvit Road, such as **Bed Supperclub** (▷ 90) or **Koi** (▷ 93).

Evening Finish the night in one of the city's many clubs (▷ 46, 90, 91), or try out one of the great jazz cafés like **Noriega's** (▷ 65).

Top 25

▶ ▶ ▶

Abhisek Dusit Throne Hall ▷ 73 King Rama V's throne hall has a distinctly Moorish feel.

Baan Jim Thompson ▷ 74 Traditional Thai architecture, lovely gardens and a tale of mystery.

Baan Kam Thieng ▷ 76 A stilt house containing everyday items showing the lifestyle of 160 years ago.

Wat Traimit ▷ 57 Immensely popular for its 10ft (3m) high, 13th-century Buddha, made of solid gold.

Wat Saket ▷ 41 Climb to the top for some of the best views of the Royal City.

Wat Ra Kang ▷ 40 Pretty temple by the river with some fine carvings and murals.

Wat Prayoon ▷ 38 A temple complex with many pagodas and a pond containing thousands of turtles.

Wat Phra Kaeo ▷ 36 The temple, which is home to the venerated Emerald Buddha, is Thailand's major Buddhist site.

Wat Pho ▷ 34 This working temple conceals a giant reclining Buddha in shining gold. It is Thailand's largest *wat*.

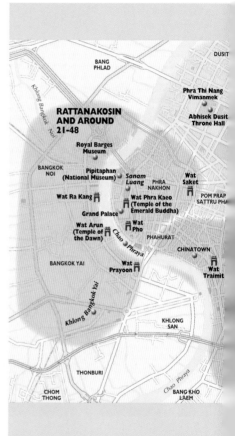

Wat Arun ▷ 32 The Temple of Dawn is wonderful when seen from the river at sunset.

Wang Suan Pakkad ▷ 81 Gardens that contain the Lacquer Pavilion and other treasures.

Thanon Sukhumvit ▷ 80 Snarled up with traffic, this road has some serious shopping outlets.

ESSENTIAL BANGKOK **TOP 25**

These pages are a quick guide to the Top 25, which are described in more detail later. Here they are listed alphabetically, and the tinted background shows which area they are in.

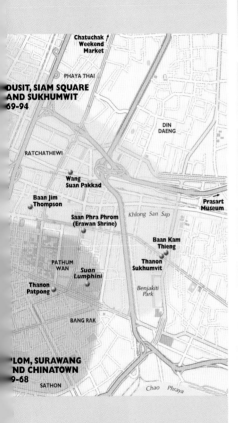

DUSIT, SIAM SQUARE
AND SUKHUMWIT
69–94

PHAYA THAI

RATCHATHEWI

Chatuchak Weekend Market

DIN DAENG

Wang Suan Pakkad

Baan Jim Thompson

Saan Phra Phrom (Erawan Shrine)

Khlong San Sap

Prasart Museum

Baan Kam Thieng

PATHUM WAN

Suan Lumphini

Thanon Sukhumvit

Thanon Patpong

Benjakiti Park

BANG RAK

LOM, SURAWANG
ND CHINATOWN
9–68

SATHON

Chao Phraya

◄ ◄ ◄

Shopping

With several megamalls to choose from, as well as weekend and night markets, you can shop round the clock. Handwoven silks, traditional crafts, designer wear and trendy Oriental design or spa products offer almost endless choice. Shopping in Bangkok is exhilarating but can be utterly exhausting, and then there is the headache of whether you can cram it all in your baggage allowance on the plane.

Bargain Buys

It's hard to resist bargains. Traditional markets are bursting with exotic produce and well-made handicrafts. Ultrasmart shopping malls stock the latest from Prada or Louis Vuitton (albeit only in tiny Asian sizes) as well as new local designers. If you don't find the clothes, shoes or furniture you want, you can have it made within a few days. Fabrics are a good buy. Thai silk comes in several weights and a variety of rich and subtle colors and patterns. HM Queen Sirikit has made great efforts to promote Mudmee, the hand-woven silk produced in Northeastern Thailand. The Phahurat area is lined with shops selling Indian silks and synthetics, while cotton fabrics, batiks and traditional Thai cotton clothing are sold at the Chatuchak Weekend Market (▷ 98).

Traditional Items

Good crafts, locally made or imported from neighboring Laos, Cambodia or Myanmar, come in a great selection at specialist shops and

SHOP 'TIL YOU DROP

Siam Paragon shopping mall (▷ 86) has smart Western designer labels and Thai design and crafts. Several young Thai designers have stores on Siam Square, a teenage heaven for wacky jewelry and accessories. Sukhumvit Road is the place to go for good tailors and for stalls selling everything from fake designer brands to DVDs and Thai silk products. Khao San Road is good for inexpensive clothes, CDs and jewelry. The best all-round place for crafts, clothes and antiques is the Chatuchak Weekend Market (▷ 98).

Buy from street markets and elegant malls

markets. The inexpensive triangular pillows (*mawn khaan*) make great gifts, although they are heavy and bulky to carry back. Benjarong, traditional royal Thai porcelain, is covered in brightly glazed enamel and used as food containers or serving dishes. You can buy simple but fine celadon, glazed pottery that comes in jade green, purple, blue and brown. Nielloware, silver objects inlaid with niello, and bronze and hand-beaten brassware are other good buys.

Authentic Antiques

Although fine antiques from all over the region are available in Bangkok, don't expect bargains. The best and priciest objects can be found at the River City Shopping Complex (▷ 63); better value can be found at the Chatuchak Weekend Market. Reputable shops will help you get the necessary export permit for most antiques. Otherwise you must apply for a license from the Fine Arts Department at the Ministry of Culture (tel 0 2422 8943).

Jewels Galore

Jewelry and cut or uncut gems, particularly blue sapphires and rubies, are excellent value. You need to know what you are buying—sometimes tinted glass is passed off as gems. Reputable jewelers belong to "The Jewel Fest Club" and will issue a certificate of authenticity and a guarantee to refund (less 10 percent) if goods are returned within 30 days. Pay with a credit card.

SPA DELIGHTS

With the booming spa culture comes a large range of spa products made in Thailand with Oriental spices and perfumes. The products are good quality, wonderful value and make for a nice present back home. The better-known brands are THANN, HARRN and the chic Pañpuri. The Thann Sanctuary in Bangkok was chosen as one of the best spas in the world. All of these brands have shops in the Emporium and Siam Paragon as well as in other shopping malls in the city.

Clothes, fabrics and antiques are good buys

Shopping by Theme

Whether you're looking for a mall, a department store, a quirky boutique, or something in between, you'll find it all in Bangkok. On this page shops are listed by theme. For a more detailed write-up, see the individual listings in Bangkok by Area.

Bangkok by Night

Until a few years ago, Bangkok did not sleep, but now a 2am closing time has been imposed on bars and nightclubs to clean up its nightlife. The Thai element of *sanuk* (fun, pleasure) that drove the wild nightlife scene before is still there, however.

Bars and Nightclubs

Most locals prefer to hang out in the city's many bars, often with live music and usually with food. Arty students and backpackers hang around the lively scene in Banglamphu. Silom Road attracts mainly local workers and foreigners and it has some excellent bar-restaurants. The *soi* (lanes) off Sukhumvit Road are mostly where the smarter bars and restaurants are found, except for the rather sleazy Nana Plaza and Soi Cowboy.

An Evening Stroll

Walk through Patpong (▷ 56) and Silom Road's night market. Watch out for the cheap fakes, from Rolexes, T-shirts and DVDs to the latest Gameboy games and Vuitton suitcases. Khao San and Banglamphu also make for a good evening stroll.

Romantic Bangkok

For a romantic alfresco meal take a dinner cruise on the Chao Phraya River (▷ 26) and see the floodlit Grand Palace and Wat Arun, or have dinner on the terrace of one of the five-star hotels overlooking the river.

Bangkok's nightlife has plenty to offer

WHAT'S ON

Bangkok's excellent English-language daily newspapers—*Bangkok Post* and *The Nation*—have listings of all cultural events as well as news and reviews of new restaurants, venues and attractions. The monthly *Bangkok 101* magazine, available from bookshops, is good for listings as well as notices about new bars, restaurants or shops. Several free listings magazines, including *Where*, *Big Chilli* and *BK Magazine,* can be found in trendy bars and restaurants. Tickets can be booked at www.thaiticketmaster.com.

Eating Out

Eating is one of the great pleasures in Bangkok. Thais eat out several times a day. Thai food is delicious once you get used to the exuberant use of chilies. Restaurants cater to every budget, and the range of foods is fantastic: from a great spicy seafood curry at a roadside stall to black cod at a trendy Sukhumvit eatery.

Thai Cuisine

Thai food is a mixture of indigenous cooking fused with some Chinese and Indian styles. It can be chili-fueled or bland depending on the region where it originated. It typically uses lemongrass and galangal, which give that special Thai taste. Coconut thickens the sauce and adds its own richness, while lime leaves, fresh cilantro (coriander) leaves, Thai basil and whole fresh peppercorns usually end up in there, too. A milder option is authentic Chinese restaurants—or the stalls in Chinatown (▷ 52).

Where to Eat

The areas with the greatest concentration of quality restaurants with menus in English are to be found around Thanon Sukhumvit and Thanon Silom. Many of the best restaurants, especially ones serving non-Thai cuisine, are in good hotels, while the best-value places to eat are food courts and at street stands. In and around Thanon Khao San in Banglamphu there are also inexpensive places to enjoy good food. If you are shopping in one of the big malls, try their popular food courts, usually located in the basement.

THE LOVE OF FOOD

Thais love eating, as is obvious from the wide selection of restaurants in Bangkok—it is claimed that there are more than 50,000, and that's not counting the foodstalls that set up on every street and the food boats along the canals. You won't go hungry, that's for sure. But if your heart is set on one particular restaurant, be sure to make a reservation—others might feel the same way about it.

Enjoy Thai cuisine in sleek restaurants and street cafés

Restaurants by Cuisine

There are restaurants to suit all tastes and budgets in Bangkok. On this page they are listed by cuisine. For a more detailed description of each restaurant, see Bangkok by Area.

American
Sheepshank Public House
▷ 48

Asian
Eat Me ▷ 66
Vertigo ▷ 68
Vientiane Kitchen ▷ 94

Cajun
Bourbon Street ▷ 92

Chinese
Mei Jiang ▷ 67

French
Aubergine ▷ 66
Le Café Siam ▷ 66
Crêpes & Co. ▷ 92
Le Normandie ▷ 68

Indian
Dosa King ▷ 92
Indus ▷ 93
Rang Mahal ▷ 94

International
Horizon River Cruise
▷ 67
The Capital by Water
Library ▷ 66
Greyhound Café ▷ 93
Kuppa ▷ 93
Vanilla Industry Restaurant
▷ 94

Italian
Enoteca Italiana ▷ 92
Govinda ▷ 93

Japanese
Koi ▷ 93
Nippon Tei ▷ 94

Mediterranean
Seven Spoons ▷ 48

Seafood
Je Ngor ▷ 93
Lord Jim ▷ 67
Pierside Seafood
Restaurant ▷ 68
Silom Village ▷ 68

Thai
Ana's Garden ▷ 92
Baan Khanitha ▷ 66
Ban Khun Mae ▷ 92
Basil ▷ 92
Blue Elephant ▷ 66
Celadon ▷ 66
Chote Chitr ▷ 48
Deck by the River ▷ 48
Harmonique ▷ 67
Hemlock ▷ 48
Laicram ▷ 93
The Loft (panel, ▷ 92)
Loy Nava ▷ 67
Le Lys ▷ 67
Mahanaga ▷ 94
Mango Tree ▷ 67
May Kaidee's Vegetarian
Restaurant ▷ 48
Nahm ▷ 67
Praya Dining ▷ 48
Ruen Mallika ▷ 94
Ruen Urai ▷ 68
Saladaeng Café ▷ 68
Salathip ▷ 68
The Spice Market ▷ 94
Sweet Basil ▷ 68

Top Tips For...

These great suggestions will help you tailor your ideal visit to Bangkok, no matter how you choose to spend your time. Each sight or listing has a fuller write-up elsewhere in the book.

A LAZY MORNING

Have a leisurely breakfast on the terrace of the Mandarin Oriental Hotel (▷ 112).

Go for an early morning stroll in Lumphini Park (▷ 54) and watch masses of Thais do their daily t'ai chi routines.

Take a long-tail boat on Khlong Bangkok Yai (▷ 100) to escape the city noise.

PAMPERING

Spend the day or the weekend being pampered at The Oriental Spa (▷ 58).

Make a traditional massage part of your visit to Wat Pho (▷ 46).

If your feet are weary from all the sightseeing, head to one of the many side-street spas in the Sukhumvit and Silom Road areas for a wonderful one-hour reflexology massage (▷ 64, 65, 91).

Relax on the river and at a calming spa (above)

SHOPPING SPREES

The Chatuchak Weekend Market (▷ 98) has more than you can bargain for, and is now easily reached by Skytrain.

The Siam Paragon (▷ 86) is one of the city's most glamorous shopping malls, with a huge cinema complex and food court.

Siam Square is full of tiny individual boutiques and narrow alleys filled with teenage chic. It has more character than the shopping malls and it's a great place to people-watch (▷ 86–88).

Markets offer great value and a huge variety of produce and goods, while the malls are increasingly sophisticated (above right and right)

Kite-flying is a popular leisure activity (below); Wat Phra Kaeo (center)

CULTURE TRAILS

See one of the few houses in the city to survive World War II at the Museum for Bangkokians (▷ 58), and understand more about the people of Bangkok.
Take a walk in old Rattanakosin (▷ 44).
Head for the quiet of Kukrit Pramoj Museum (▷ 58), set in peaceful gardens.

TEMPLES

It's a must to go and see Wat Phra Kaeo (▷ 36), home to the very sacred Emerald Buddha.
Throw coins in the bowls for good luck and have a traditional massage at Wat Pho (▷ 34).
See the sun set over Wat Arun (▷ 32).

GREEN SPACES

Practice t'ai chi in Lumphini Park (▷ 54), go for a stroll or row a boat on the lake.
Admire the kite-flying skills as exotic shapes swoop overhead at Sanam Luang (▷ 30) and teams with fighting kites show off.
Cycle on the narrow pathways along the Thonburi *khlongs* (▷ 100) through villages with stilt houses set in gardens.

Thonburi (above); Lumphini Park (below)

BUDGET ROOMS

Villa Guest House (▷ 109) is an old teak house where you don't wake up to the noise of a traffic jam, but to the crowing of roosters.
The Atlanta (▷ 109) has achieved legendary status among the city's cheap sleeps.

ESSENTIAL BANGKOK TOP TIPS FOR...

CHILDREN'S ACTIVITIES

A long-tail boat on the canals (below); Erawan Shrine (center)

Kids love speeding along the river and into the canals on the brightly decorated long-tail boats (▷ 100, 118).

Young children will love the animals, feeding times and entertainment at Safari World (▷ 103).

Older children will love Mahboonkrong (MBK) Center (▷ 87), with loud pop music, food stalls, cheap clothing and a whole floor dedicated to mobile phones and decorations and accessories.

BEING THRIFTY

It's not entirely free, but very inexpensive, to hop on a river ferry just before sunset when Bangkok looks ageless and beautiful.

See the best of Thai contemporary art at the Thavibu Art Gallery (ATC Jewelry Trade Center, 4th Floor, Suite 433, 919/1 Thanon Silom, tel 0 2266 5454, www.thavibu.com).

Watch the crowds make offerings at the Erawan Shrine (▷ 78) and pay for traditional Thai dancers.

GREAT VIEWS

Sip a cocktail on one of the world's highest roof terraces, aptly named Vertigo (▷ 65, 68).

Take a room at the Peninsula Hotel (▷ 112) and see the city in all its glory.

The Peninsula Hotel (above); view from Wat Saket (below)

View the grandeur of the royal city of Rattanakosin from up high on one of the glorious golden *chedi* on the Golden Mount near Wat Saket (▷ 41).

Bangkok by Area

Rattanakosin is the sacred heart of Bangkok, with some of the country's holiest of holy monuments.

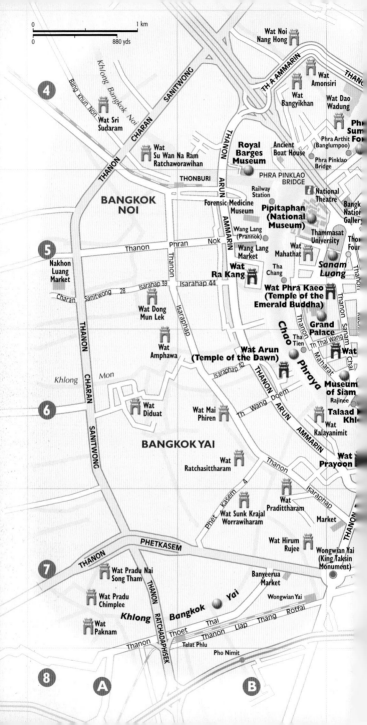

Wat Noi
Nang Hong

TH A AMMARIN

Wat
Amonsiri

Wat
Bangyikhan

Wat Dao
Wadung

Phra
Sum
Fo

Khlong Bangkok Noi

Bang Khun Non

Wat Sri
Sudaram

CHARAN

SANITWONG

Phra Arthit
(Banglumpoo)

Wat
Su Wan Na Ram
Ratchaworawihan

Royal
Barges
Museum

Ancient
Boat House

Phra Pinklao
Bridge

THANON

ARUN

THONBURI

PHRA PINKLAO
BRIDGE

Railway
Station

National
Theatre

BANGKOK
NOI

AMMARIN

Forensic
Medicine
Museum

Pipitaphan
(National
Museum)

Bang
Nation
Gallery

Wang Lang
(Prannok)

Thammasat
University

Thor
Foun

Wat
Mahathat

5

Thanon

Phran

Nok

Wang Lang
Market

Sanam
Luang

Nakhon
Luang
Market

Wat
Ra Kang

Tha
Chang

Thanon

CHARAN

SANITWONG

Charan Sanitwong 28

Isarahap 39

Isarahap 44

Wat Phra Kaeo
(Temple of the
Emerald Buddha)

Isaraphap

Wat Dong
Mun Lek

Chao

Grand
Palace

Thanon

Sanam

Wat
Cha

Wat
Amphawa

Tha
Tien

Th Thai Wang

6

Khlong

Mon

Wat Arun
(Temple of the Dawn)

Phraya

Wat
Diduat

Isarahap 42

THANON

ARUN

Museum
of Siam

Rajinee

Wat Mai
Phiren

Th. Wang Doem

Talaad
Khl

BANGKOK YAI

Wat
Kalayanimit

AMMARIN

Wat
Ratchasittharam

Thanon

Wat
Prayoon

Isaraphap

Phet Kasem 4

Wat
Praditharam

Market

THANON

Wat Sunk Krajal
Worrawiharam

Wat Hirum
Rujee

Wongwian Yai
(King Taksin
Monument)

PHETKASEM

7

THANON

Wat Pradu Nai
Song Tham

Banyeerua
Market

Wat Pradu
Chimplee

Khlong

Bangkok

Yai

Wongwian Yai

Wat
Paknam

SANITWONG

THANON

RATCHADAPHISEK

Thoet

Thai

Thanon

Liap

Thang

Rotfai

Thanon

Talat Phlu

Pho Nimit

8

A

B

0   1 km
0   880 yds

4

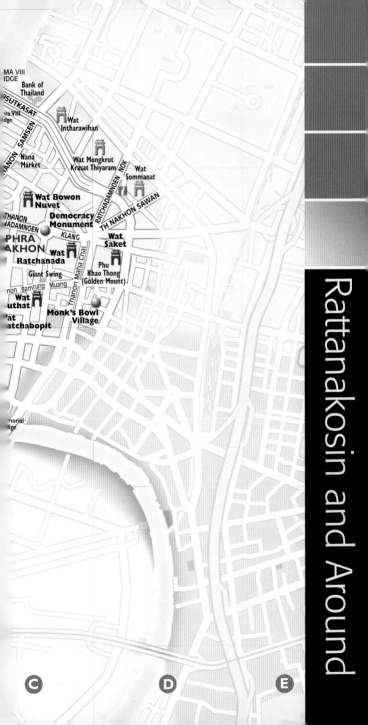

MA VIII
IDGE

Bank of
Thailand

'SUTKASAT

ma VIII
idge

Wat
Intharawihan

THANON SAMSEN

Nana
Market

Wat Mongkrut
Krasat Thiyaram

Wat
Sommanat

RATCHADAMNOEN NOK

TH NAKHON SAWAN

THANON
ADAMNOEN

Wat Bowon
Nuvet

Democracy
Monument

PHRA
AKHON

KLANG

Wat
Saket

Wat
Ratchanada

Thanon Maha Chai

Phu
Khao Thong
(Golden Mount)

Giant Swing

non Bamrung Muang

Wat
uthat

Monk's Bowl
Village

at
atchabopit

norial
idge

C

D

E

Grand Palace

TOP 25

HIGHLIGHTS

- Chakri Maha Prasad
- The garden
- Wat Phra Kaeo Museum
- Amarin Vinichai Prasad (Coronation Hall)
- Dusit Maha Prasad

TIP

- Ignore anyone around the Grand Palace who, telling you that it is closed for the day, offers what will turn out to be a shopping tour of the city.

The palace, home to the Thai royal family until 1946, is undoubtedly grand, with so many jewels cramped into a small area. The effect is overwhelming.

The oldest building When King Rama I moved from Thonburi to Rattanakosin his plan was to construct an exact copy of Ayutthaya. First he built himself a palace and a royal temple, Wat Phra Kaeo (▷ 36). The oldest buildings are the Maha Montien and the Dusit Maha Prasad, the first brick building (1789) constructed in typical Thai style. It is now the resting place for deceased royals before their cremation (▷ 30).

The foreigner The magnificent Chakri Maha Prasad, designed by British architects, is often referred to as "the *farang* (foreigner) with the

Clockwise from far left: Yak Temple guardian; the exterior of the palace; Ramakien murals in the Wat Phra Kaeo Museum; detail of the exterior; the grounds; soldiers changing the guard

chada (headdress worn by Thai dancers)," as the main building, in imperial Victorian style, is topped with three Thai spires. The ground level houses a display of weapons, while on the next level are the Throne Hall and Reception Hall. Note that only the weapons display is open to the public.

Model changes Within the palace complex is the Wat Phra Kaeo Museum which houses tiny Buddha images in precious materials and models showing alterations that have been made to the palace and Wat Phra Kaeo from their beginnings to the modern day. The Amarin Vinichai Prasad (Coronation Hall), built by Rama I and expanded by Rama II and III, is part of the Maha Montien, and is traditionally the room in which each king spends the night after his coronation.

THE BASICS

www.palaces.thai.net

➕ B5–C5

✉ Thanon Na Phra Lan

☎ 0 2623 5500

🕐 Daily 8.30–4.30

🚤 Tha Chang pier

♿ Good

✋ Expensive; includes Grand Palace, Queen Sirikit Textile Museum, Wat Phra Kaeo and Vimanmek Palace

❓ Modest dress—no shorts, vests, short skirts, flip-flops or sandals (without ankle straps). Clothes can be rented at the office. Audio guides available

Mae Nam Chao Phraya

Long-tail boat (left);
nighttime river
transportation (below)

THE BASICS

☷ B6

🍽 Excellent restaurants and bars

🚤 Public express boats, private long-tail boats

♿ None

❓ The Chao Phraya Express Boat Company offers special tours on their boats and a map of the sights along the way. Info Center at Central Pier (Tha Saphan Taksin)
☎ 0 2866 3163

HIGHLIGHTS

● Several *wats*, including Wat Arun
● Grand Palace
● Several hotels, including the Oriental
● 19th-century buildings
● Rice barges being towed to and from Bangkok's port
● People living alongside the river
● Fresher air, a breeze and no traffic jams

The Chao Phraya River, Bangkok's main artery, is a wonderful balm. To board a boat, sniff the breeze and see the grand buildings lining the banks is one of the most exciting and soothing experiences in Bangkok.

The river of kings You can learn much about the history of Bangkok from the Chao Phraya, for the city was designed to be seen from the water: A hundred years ago you would have arrived upriver from the sea port rather than across the city from the airport. Besides the Grand Palace, look out for other royal buildings: the Royal Barges Museum, Chakrabongse House, Wat Ra Kang, Silpakorn University and, between Krung Thon and Phra Pokklao bridges, the childhood home of Queen Sirikit.

The river of the people The more congested road traffic becomes, the more people in Bangkok dream of returning to their river. Many inhabitants still live waterborne lives in stilt houses and on barges, dependent on the brown river for their washing, fishing and transportation. Some people living on barges trade in charcoal, while others work at the rice warehouses across the river. Farther upstream, look for market traders around Pak Khlong Talaat and teak loggers with their goods moored around Krung Thon Bridge. Life carries on as it has for centuries, with only a tidemark on some buildings to mark the devastating flood of fall 2011, when hundreds of people lost their lives.

Pipitaphan (National Museum)

You'll need as long as possible to come to terms with this astonishing collection of Thai art and archaeology. Most of the museum's buildings, too, are works of art in their own right.

Oldest letters The visit starts with a useful introduction to Thai history. Note the black-stone inscription from Sukhothai, the oldest-known record of the Thai alphabet. Two modern buildings house the main collection of pre-Thai and Thai sculpture, as well as pieces from elsewhere in Asia. An important exhibit in the southern wing is one of the earliest images of Buddha, from Gandhara in India. A garage in a nearby building houses the collection of magnificent royal funeral chariots, including the amazing *Vejayant Rajarot*, built by Rama I in 1785 and still occasionally used, even though it needs 300 men to pull it.

Palace of Wang Na Built in the 1780s as a home for the king's successor, the palace houses a magnificent collection of Thai art objects. Note the collection of traditional musical instruments from Southeast Asia.

Buddhaisawan Chapel The Phra Sihing Buddha here is said to have been divinely created in Sri Lanka and sent to Sukhothai in the 13th century. Despite doubts about its origins (it dates from the 15th century), it is still worshiped by many and is carried in procession at the Thai New Year.

THE BASICS

+ B5
- Thanon Naphratad 1
- 0 2224 1370
- Usually Wed–Sun 9–4, but check in advance
- Café
- Tha Phra Chan
- Few
- Inexpensive
- Free English tours from the ticket pavilion on Wed at 9.30am (Buddhism) and Thu 9.30am (Thai art and culture)

HIGHLIGHTS

- Sukhothai sculpture
- *Vejayant Rajarot* chariot
- Red House
- Royal funeral chariots
- Murals in the Buddhaisawan Chapel

TIP

- Photography is not allowed inside the museum.

Royal Barges Museum

Thai kings regularly used these splendidly carved barges, but now they are only taken out during the barge procession. This event marks a nonannual, auspicious Buddhist calendar year.

Fit for a king These superb boats are a reminder that Bangkok was once all canals. The most majestic is the king's personal barge, the *Suphannahong*, or the golden swan, which was the mythical steed of the Hindu god Brahma. The 148ft (45m) longboat is intricately carved from the trunk of a single teak tree and its prow rears up into a swanlike bird, known as the *hongsa*. The barge, manned by 50 oarsmen, was launched by King Rama VI in 1911. The second-largest barge in the shed is the *Anantanagaraj*. It is beautifully carved and

Detail of the heavily decorated golden Anantanagaraj *(left); the magnificent* Suphannahong *(below), the king's personal barge*

has a seven-headed *naga* serpent at its prow. Around it are others from the royal fleet—when 19th-century Thai kings ventured out, they were accompanied by hundreds of vessels.

The Royal Barge Procession No new royal barges have been built, but the spectacular pageant on water still occasionally takes place. Originally, the large fleet of royal barges aligned on the rivers and canals at the island capital of Ayutthaya at the end of the rainy season, when the king offered new robes for the monks at the royal monasteries. This event is still the main reason for the procession, but only in auspicious years. However, it can take place to celebrate another event, such as the King's birthday in 2012 when 52 barges set sail—a majestic vision on the water.

THE BASICS

- B4
- 80/1 Soi Rim Khlong Bangkok Noi
- 0 2424 0004
- Daily 9–5
- Chao Phraya Express boat to Tha Wang Lang and then taxi to museum
- Few
- Inexpensive

Sanam Luang

Kites are sold at Sanam Luang and enjoyed by old and young alike

THE BASICS

➕ B5–C5

✉ Thanon Ratchadamnoen Nai

🕐 Daily morning–evening

🍴 Foodstalls, food market

🚤 Express boat to Tha Chang and then a 10-minute walk

♿ Few

💲 Free

❓ Often Thai traditional dance can be seen at Lak Muang

DID YOU KNOW?

● Every Thai city has a foundation stone representing the city spirit *(phii muang)*.

● Many buildings have a spirit house, a small version of a traditional Thai house, where the guardian spirit is said to reside.

● An unusual shrine near the Swissotel in Nai Lert Park (➕ F5/6) contains a spirit house and several huge wooden phalluses.

Just north of the Grand Palace are the royal cremation grounds, today most often used for picnics. It's a good place to relax after sightseeing, or to watch the kite competitions that usually take place between February and May.

Royal cremation grounds This vast green field near the Grand Palace was originally designed as the funeral grounds for royal members of the Chakri Dynasty. The last ceremonial cremation, attended by thousands of people, took place in 2012 for the funeral of Princess Bejaratana Rajasuda, the King's cousin. Sanam Luang is also the site of the annual Royal Plowing Ceremony (▷ 114), a Brahmanic tradition, when the king marks the beginning of the rice-growing season, and for the celebrations of King Bhumibol's birthday on December 5 (▷ 114). The statue of the earth goddess, Mae Thorani, in a pavilion on the northern side, was erected by King Chulalongkorn.

Lak Muang (City Pillar Shrine) This lovely shrine, believed to be inhabited by the spirit that protects Bangkok, is built around two Sivaite *lingam* wooden pillars erected by Rama I in 1782 to mark the founding of his new capital. Thais believe their wishes will be granted if they worship at the shrine, and that it has powers to grant fertility to those who come to make offerings of pig heads and incense. Thai dancers are commissioned to perform and to thank the deities for granting a wish.

Wat Arun

HIGHLIGHTS

● Central *prang*
● Close-up of the Chinese porcelain decoration on the *prangs*
● Main Buddha image inside the *bot*
● Murals inside the *bot*

TIP

● Boat tours restrict your time at Wat Arun but the cross-river ferries are frequent and give you more freedom.

Despite the competition from many skyscrapers on Bangkok's skyline, the glittering towers of the Temple of Dawn rise tall above the river.

The temple of Arun King Taksin chose this 17th-century *wat* for his royal temple and palace as it was the first place in Thonburi to catch the morning light. The Emerald Buddha was housed here after it was recaptured from Laos, before being moved to Wat Phra Kaeo in 1785. Even without the sacred statue, Wat Arun continued to be much revered, and the kings Rama II and Rama III reconstructed and enlarged it to its present height of 220ft (67m). Today, the *wat* has a long, elongated, Khmer-style *prang* (tower), and four minor towers, symbolizing Mount Meru, the terrestrial representation of

The towering prang of Wat Arun is covered with Chinese porcelain (left); monks visit the wat (middle); a statue decorated with an offering (below)

the 33 heavens. The *prangs* are covered with pieces of porcelain, which Chinese boats coming to Bangkok used as ballast.

The main *prang* Steep steps lead to the two terraces that form the base of the *prang*. The different layers, or heavens, are supported by *kinnari*, or half-humans, and frightening *yakshas*, or demons. Pavilions on the first platform contain statues of the Buddha at important stages of his life, while on the second terrace four statues of the Hindu god Indra stand guard.

Quiet stroll Stroll around the compound and have a look at the interior of the *bot* (chapel). The main Buddha image inside is believed to have been designed by Rama II himself, but the murals date from the reign of Rama V.

THE BASICS

www.watarun.net

+ B6

✉ 34 Thanon Arun Amarin, Bangkok Yai

☎ 0 2891 1149

🕐 Daily 8.30–5.30. Note: ongoing renovation work until 2016

🍴 Foodstalls on the riverbank

🚢 Express boat to Tha Tien pier, then cross-river ferry to Wat Arun

♿ None

💷 Inexpensive

Wat Pho

After a visit to the Grand Palace or a day's shopping, there's nothing as relaxing as a visit to the beautiful temple compound of Wat Pho and a good Thai massage to get you back on your feet.

The Reclining Buddha Wat Pho was built in the 16th century during the Ayutthaya period and almost completely rebuilt in 1781 by Rama I. It is Bangkok's oldest and Thailand's largest *wat*. Thanon Chethuphon divides the grounds in two, but only the northern part is open to the public. The temple's main attraction is the 19th-century giant Reclining Buddha, 151ft (46m) long and 49ft (15m) high, which represents the dying Buddha in the position he adopted to attain nirvana. The soles of the feet are decorated in mother-of-pearl with 108

Clockwise from far left: With a saffron-colored umbrella to match his robes, a monk crosses the sunny courtyard; the exterior shaded by trees; small towers surround the buildings of Wat Pho; Chinese figures guarding the gate; detail of Ramakien bas-relief in marble; Reclining Buddha

signs of Buddha. The beautiful *bot*, or central shrine, has delicately carved sandstone panels representing the *Ramakien* and the finest mother-of-pearl inlaid doors. Although Wat Pho contains 91 *chedis*, the four most important are dedicated to the first Chakri kings. Visitors can acquire merit by putting a coin in each of the 108 bronze bowls.

Center of learning Rama III wanted this temple to be used for education, and Thais still consider it their first public university. The murals in the *viharn* and other buildings explain a variety of subjects, such as religion, geography, yoga, astrology, science and arts. Today, the temple complex still includes the traditional Thai Massage School (▷ 46), which teaches the art of Thai massage and herbal remedies.

THE BASICS

www.watpho.com

✚ C6

✉ 2 Thanon Sanam Chai

☎ 0 2225 9595

🕐 Daily 8–6.30, massage 8–5

🚢 Tha Tien pier

♿ Good

💰 Moderate

Wat Phra Kaeo

HIGHLIGHTS

● Murals in the Chapel Royal
● The Emerald Buddha
● Mural of the *Ramakien*

TIPS

● Dress modestly and cover arms and legs.
● Sandals without ankle straps and flip-flops are not permitted for foreigners.
● Sarongs are on loan at the entrance.

The Temple of the Emerald Buddha reveals some of the most stunning architecture in all Southeast Asia and demonstrates the tradition of firm belief the Thai people have in Buddism and in their nation.

The Emerald Buddha Wat Phra Kaeo is the holiest of all Thai *wats*, and the small green-jade statue of the Buddha, high on its golden altar in the Chapel Royal, is the most sacred image in Thailand. It was first found in 1464 and years later several miracles occurred, giving the Buddha a reputation for bringing good fortune. The late Ayutthaya-style murals on the surrounding walls depict the lives of Buddha, and the superb door panels with mother-of-pearl inlay illustrate scenes from

Clockwise from far left: A bejeweled, painted temple guard; a sala (open-sided rest pavilion); golden stupa and stone chedis; a statue with a blue-painted face supports part of the building; golden statue of a clothed Buddha set before the green and orange-glazed tiled, tiered roof; rose-pink Khmer-style prangs; worshipers at the shrine

the *Ramakien*, the Thai version of the Indian *Ramayana*. The golden outer walls and gilded angels reflect the sun, while bells along the roofline give voice to the wind. The Museum of the Temple of the Emerald Buddha houses the exquisite collection of royal costumes for this sacred statue, made from precious metals and jewels.

More temples On the upper terrace next to the Chapel Royal are three other very sacred buildings: the Royal Pantheon, surrounded by gilded *kinaree* (male) and *kinara* (female) half-human figures; the Library, which holds the *Tripitaka*, the sacred Buddhist scriptures; and the golden Phra Si Ratana pagoda, which houses ashes of Buddha. The whole ground is enclosed by galleries decorated with murals.

THE BASICS

www.palaces.thai.net

✚ B5–C5

✉ Thanon Na Phra Lan

☎ 0 2623 5500

🕐 Daily 8.30–3.30

🚢 Tha Chang pier

♿ None

✋ Included in entrance to Grand Palace

Wat Prayoon

● Just upstream of Memorial Bridge is the Catholic Church of Santa Cruz, the core of the old Portuguese quarter.

● Several Portuguese churches still exist today, including the Church of the Immaculate Conception (1847) near Krung Thon Bridge and the Holy Rosary Church (1787).

This temple complex in the shadow of the old Memorial Bridge seems surreal, with its giant *chedi*, the artificial hill covered with miniature shrines to loved ones and a pool alive with turtles partial to the taste of tourists' fingers (be warned).

Distinctive pagodas Wat Prayoon, also called Temple of the Dawn and known locally under its longer name of Wat Prayun Rawongsawat, was built during the reign of Rama III by the powerful local Bunnag family. Its huge *chedis* (pagodas) are easily recognized from the river and Memorial Bridge. In 2007 the pagoda underwent a huge renovation and now appears white. The *wat* has some fine mother-of-pearl inlaid doors.

Detail of the richly decorated overhanging roof and gable (left); the exterior of Wat Prayoon (below)

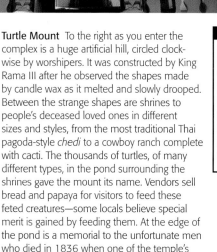

Turtle Mount To the right as you enter the complex is a huge artificial hill, circled clockwise by worshipers. It was constructed by King Rama III after he observed the shapes made by candle wax as it melted and slowly drooped. Between the strange shapes are shrines to people's deceased loved ones in different sizes and styles, from the most traditional Thai pagoda-style *chedi* to a cowboy ranch complete with cacti. The thousands of turtles, of many different types, in the pond surrounding the shrines gave the mount its name. Vendors sell bread and papaya for visitors to feed these feted creatures—some locals believe special merit is gained by feeding them. At the edge of the pond is a memorial to the unfortunate men who died in 1836 when one of the temple's cannons exploded.

THE BASICS

🕂 C6

✉ Soi 1, off Thanon Thetsaban, Thonburi

🕐 Daily 6–6

🚢 Tha Saphan Phut Memorial Bridge

♿ None

🎫 Free; inexpensive turtle food

Wat Ra Kang

Wall paintings (left and middle); the gardens (below)

THE BASICS

⊞ B5

✉ Soi Wat Rakang Khositaram, off Thanon Arun Amarin

🕐 Daily 7am–9pm

🚤 Express boat to Tha Chang pier, then cross-river ferry to Wat Ra Kang pier

♿ None

✋ Free

HIGHLIGHTS

● Wood carvings in the library
● Murals of the *Ramakien*
● Views of the Grand Palace

Claims that the Ayutthaya period was one of the high points of Thai art are supported by this undervisited temple, set on the banks of the Phraya river. Its murals and wood carvings are exceptionally fine.

Bell temple Most visitors overlook this delightful smaller *wat*, which dates from the Ayutthaya period, as does its neighbor Wat Arun (▷ 32). King Taksin undertook serious restorations when he settled in Thonburi, and Rama I rebuilt it extensively. *Rakang* means bell, and visitors can ring the bells to bring good luck. The lovely garden feels far removed from bustling Bangkok and is a great place to rest, to enjoy the cross-river view of the Grand Palace, or even to meditate.

A royal present The beautiful library on the compound of Wat Ra Kang was a gift from Rama I to the temple after he founded the Chakri Dynasty. He lived in this elegant 18th-century teak building before he became king, and carried out extensive renovations at the time. The stucco and carved wooden doors and window panels are incredibly fine examples of the Ayutthaya style, depicting figures from the epic *Ramakien*, the Thai interpretation of the Indian Hindu *Ramayana* story. Both the doors and the murals on the interior walls—the work of the great priest-painter Phra Acharn Nak—are considered by art historians to be among the finest in Bangkok.

A decorated window (below); the Golden Mount (right)

Wat Saket

It's easy to get lost in the grounds of this vast, peaceful temple, but the short, steep climb up the Golden Mount puts everything in perspective and offers great views over Rattanakosin and the city.

Golden Mount The main attraction of this temple is the Golden Mount (Phu Khao Thong). The artificial hill, nearly 262ft (80m) high, was created in the early 19th century after a large *chedi* built by Rama III collapsed when the underlying ground gave way. Only a huge pile of rubble was left, but as Buddhists believe that a religious building should never be destroyed, King Rama IV had 1,000 teak logs put into the foundations. Later, Rama V built a small *chedi* on top of the hill, which is believed to contain Buddha's teeth. During World War II, concrete walls were added to halt erosion. Views from the terrace on top of the hill are wonderful, and you are allowed into the golden *chedi*.

Temple complex The temple was built outside the city walls by King Rama I during the late 18th century as the city's main crematory. The king performed the Royal Hair Bathing Ceremony here before he was crowned. When plague raged through the city in the 19th century, the temple became a charnel house to tens of thousands of victims. The temple building itself is not very interesting, but the fine murals inside the main temple are worth a close inspection. There are two important old Buddha statues in the Shrine Hall.

THE BASICS

- D5
- Cakkraphatdiphong
- 0 2223 4561
- Daily 8–5.30
- Skytrain Ratchathewi, then long-tail boat to Phan Fha pier
- None
- Free; donation for top of Golden Mount

HIGHLIGHTS

- Murals in the main chapel
- Tiny bird and antiques market
- Candle-lit procession up the Golden Mount late October/early November

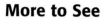

More to See

DEMOCRACY MONUMENT

This art deco monument was constructed in 1932 to commemorate Thailand's transformation from an absolute to a constitutional monarchy. The 75 cannon balls buried in the base refer to the Buddhist Year 2475, which is AD1932, and the four wings stand 78ft (24m) tall, representing June 24 when the constitution was signed. The monument is always a focal point of political protests.

➕ C5 ✉ Thanon Ratchadamnoen Klang 🚢 Tha Phra Athit

MONK'S BOWL VILLAGE

Only a few families still make the handcrafted black lacquer monks' bowls, in the last remaining of the three villages established by Rama I for this purpose. The bowls, made from steel, copper and wood, and coated with several layers of black lacquer, can also be bought here.

➕ D5 ✉ Soi Bahn Bat, off Thanon Wora Chak 🚇 Skytrain Ratchathewi then long-tail boat to Phan Fha pier

MUSEUM SIAM

www.museumsiam.org

Located in a renovated colonial building, this interactive museum depicts the history of Thailand in a fresh and innovative way. Kids will love the opportunity to dress up.

➕ C6 ✉ Thanon Sanam Chai ☎ 0225 2777 🕐 Tue–Sun 10–6 🚢 Rajinee pier 🖐 Expensive

PHRA SUMEN FORT

Dating from 1783, this is one of the 14 city fortresses built to protect the city against naval invasions. The octagonal structure is surrounded by the small Santichaiprakan Park. A walkway leads from the fort to the Phra Pin Klao Bridge, allowing you to peek inside some of the old buildings. The area of Banglamphu takes its name from the Lamphu or Engler Tree. Only one of these trees, a mangrove plant which grew all along the river, survives and is in the park.

➕ C4 ✉ Thanon Phra Athit 🕐 Daily 24 hours 🚢 Tha Phra Athit

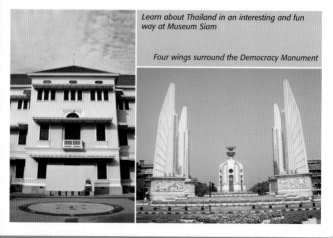

Learn about Thailand in an interesting and fun way at Museum Siam

Four wings surround the Democracy Monument

RATTANAKOSIN AND AROUND MORE TO SEE

TALAAD PAK KHLONG

Thailand's biggest, and thought to be best, flower market is one of Bangkok's most colorful and aromatic places to visit. The atmosphere in and around the stalls is frenetic in the early morning and during festival seasons, when flowers play a big part in the festivities.

➕ C6 ✉ Thanon Chak Phet, near Memorial Bridge ⏰ Daily 24 hours but most activity at night ⛴ Tha Saphan Phut ✋ Free

WAT BOWON NUVET

www.watbowon.org

This temple houses the Phra Phutthachinnasi, a very beautiful Buddha image molded around 1357. The temple is considered one of Bangkok's most important temples as King Rama IV was chief abbot here before he ascended the throne. The present king stayed for a short time in 1956.

➕ C5 ✉ Thanon Phra Sumen, Banglamphu ☎ 0 2281 2831 ⏰ Daily 8–5 ⛴ Tha Phra Athit ✋ Free ℹ Dress appropriately

WAT RATCHANADA

The strangest structure on this temple compound is Loha Prasad, or the Iron Monastery, a pink building with metal spires, spectacularly lit at night. Bangkok's biggest amulet market is held daily nearby.

➕ C5 ✉ Off Thanon Maha Chai, opposite Wat Saket ☎ 0 2224 8807 ⏰ Daily 8–5 🍴 Foodstalls ⛴ Express ferry to Tha Chang pier and then *tuk-tuk* ✋ Free

WAT SUTHAT

Wat Suthat houses a 14th-century Buddha statue surrounded by depictions of the Buddha's last 24 lives. The courtyard is filled with old statues of scholars and sailors, brought as ballast in rice boats, while the doors of the *wat* are said to have been carved by King Rama II. In an annual ceremony for the rice harvest men used to ride on the Giant Swing and try to grab a bag of silver coins hanging from a pole.

➕ C5 ✉ Off Thanon Bamrung Muang ☎ 0 2224 9845 ⏰ Daily 8.30–9 🍴 Foodstalls ⛴ Tha Chang

Three images of Buddha on the exterior of Wat Suthat

Rattanakosin (Royal City)

See where it all began, with the grandest of the city's temples, street markets, a park and maybe a relaxing massage on the way.

DISTANCE: 2 miles (3km) **ALLOW:** 3 hours excluding sights

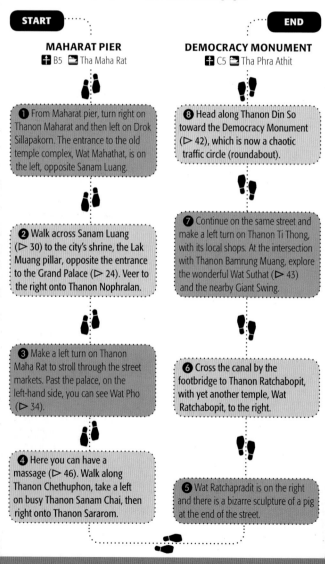

START

MAHARAT PIER
B5 🚢 Tha Maha Rat

❶ From Maharat pier, turn right on Thanon Maharat and then left on Drok Sillapakorn. The entrance to the old temple complex, Wat Mahathat, is on the left, opposite Sanam Luang.

❷ Walk across Sanam Luang (▷ 30) to the city's shrine, the Lak Muang pillar, opposite the entrance to the Grand Palace (▷ 24). Veer to the right onto Thanon Nophralan.

❸ Make a left turn on Thanon Maha Rat to stroll through the street markets. Past the palace, on the left-hand side, you can see Wat Pho (▷ 34).

❹ Here you can have a massage (▷ 46). Walk along Thanon Chethuphon, take a left on busy Thanon Sanam Chai, then right onto Thanon Sararom.

END

DEMOCRACY MONUMENT
C5 🚢 Tha Phra Athit

❽ Head along Thanon Din So toward the Democracy Monument (▷ 42), which is now a chaotic traffic circle (roundabout).

❼ Continue on the same street and make a left turn on Thanon Ti Thong, with its local shops. At the intersection with Thanon Bamrung Muang, explore the wonderful Wat Suthat (▷ 43) and the nearby Giant Swing.

❻ Cross the canal by the footbridge to Thanon Ratchabopit, with yet another temple, Wat Ratchabopit, to the right.

❺ Wat Ratchapradit is on the right and there is a bizarre sculpture of a pig at the end of the street.

Shopping

AMULET MARKET

Stalls and small shops at this outdoor market sell all kinds of amulets, from the obvious images of Buddha and famous monks and abbots to rare and valuable relics. Collectors hover like vultures over the stalls.

➕ B5 ✉ Across Wat Mahathat temple, off Thanon Maharat 🚢 Tha Chang

ELEPHANT HOUSE

www.elephant-house.com
This shop has a selection of furniture and artifacts made from traditional materials such as rattan, bamboo and lacquerware. Everything sold here is designed by the owner, Cherie Aung-Khin, and brought to life by skilled craftsmen.

➕ C7 ✉ 230/27 Soi Krungthonburi 6, Krungthonburi Road 🕿 0 2860 6920 🚇 Skytrain Krung Thonburi

LOFTY BAMBOO

www.loftybamboo.com
This is a fun shop selling gifts, bags, clothes and jewelry made by the Hmong, Lisu and Akha hill tribes. Outlets such as Lofty Bamboo encourage the continuity of these traditional skills and ensure that the villagers get a fair price for their work.

➕ C5 ✉ G–10 1st Floor Buddy Hotel, 265 Thanon Khao San, Talatyot, Phranakorn 🕿 0 2629 4716 🚢 Tha Phra Athit

NITTAYA CURRY SHOP

Nittaya's curry pastes are considered Thailand's best and her well-sealed curry pots make a perfect souvenir or gift. You can try out the preparations at the gift and snack session before you buy.

➕ C5 ✉ Thanon Chakkaphong 136–140, Banglamphu 🕿 0 2976 1600 🚢 Tha Phra Athit

SHAMAN BOOKS

www.shaman-books.tripod.com
A new and used bookshop where a vast range of novels, guide books, Buddhist titles and Asian travel literature can be found. Their computerized system can even search for specific books in stock.

➕ C5 ✉ 71 Thanon Khao San 🕿 0 2629 0418 🚢 Tha Phra Athit

SILVER PARADISE

Khao San and Thanon Tanao has become an area specializing in wholesale jewelry, and sterling silver in particular. The most amazing silver beads, pendants and gorgeous silver jewelry designs can be found here at just a little more than wholesale prices. Most items are sold by the weight, and by the amount of craftsmanship involved.

SIAM BRONZE

www.siambronze.com
The standard of Thai bronzework at Siam Bronze is extremely high. The prices are competitive also as you are able to buy some bronze tableware direct from the factory.

➕ D7 ✉ 1250 New Road, Bangrak 🕿 0 2234 9346 🚇 Skytrain Saphan Taksin 🚢 Tha Oriental

TAEKEE TAEKON

At Taekee Taekon the prices are more or less fixed—expect around a 10 percent discount—and there is a reasonable choice of quality textiles, silk items, axe cushions, jewelry, baskets, various stationery items as well as bags.

➕ C4 ✉ 118 Thanon Phra Athit 🕿 0 2629 1473 🚢 Tha Phra Athit

THANON KHAO SAN MARKET

This street is a mecca for visitors and stalls and shops are piled high with everything possible they may need and more. Expect to find henna tattooing, hemp clothing, fairy lights, T-shirts, fresh orange juice, banana pancakes and a raft of fake designer wear. Also, if you have time, check out the alleyways away from the main thoroughfare, which often have many other interesting shops.

➕ C5 ✉ Thanon Khao San 🚢 Tha Phra Athit

Entertainment and Nightlife

BROWN SUGAR

www.brownsugarbangkok.com
Brown Sugar—the Jazz
Boutique—has been
around since the 1980s
and continues to draw
great bands. The Brown
Sugar Showcase, every
last Friday and Saturday
of the month, features
international and touring
bands.

🚹 C5 ✉ 469 Wanchad
Junction, Thanon Phrasumen,
Baworniet ☎ 0 2282 0396
🕐 Tue–Thu, Sun 5pm–
12.30am, Fri–Sat 5pm–2am
🚢 Tha Phra Athit

THE CLUB KHAOSAN

www.theclubkhaosan.com
Whatever your favorite
sound, Progressive,
Electro, Trance or House,
resident and international
DJs pump it out across
the large dance floor
with their state-of-the-art
sound system. Live bands
also perform here.

🚹 C5 ✉ 123 Thanon Khao
San, Talat Yot, Phra Nakhon
☎ 0 2629 1010 🕐 Daily
10pm–3am 🚢 Tha Phra Athit

LAK MUANG

Thai dancers are commis-
sioned to perform at this
shrine (▷ 30).

🚹 B–C5 ✉ Thanon
Ratchadamnoen Nai 🚢 Tha
Phra Chan

MAY KAIDEE COOKERY CLASS

www.maykaidee.com/
cooking-school
Long-established vegetar-
ian cookery school with
morning or afternoon

sessions. Students learn
about Thai herbs and
spices, how to make
spring rolls and classic
Thai dishes such as
Pad Thai—and then eat
the results.

🚹 C5 ✉ 59 Tanao Road,
Banglamphu ☎ 0 2629 4413
🕐 Daily; classes begin at 9am
or 2pm 🚢 Tha Phra Athit

MULLIGANS IRISH BAR

www.mulligansthailand.com
Head to this lively venue
to watch live international
sport on one of the 15
televisions dotted around
the place and enjoy an
ice-cold Guinness. Pub
grub staples are avail-
able as well as Thai food.
Late-night live bands play
Monday to Saturday in
the upstairs bar.

🚹 C5 ✉ 265 Thanon Khao
San, Talat Yot, Phra Nakhon
☎ 0 2629 4477 🕐 Daily,
24-hours 🚢 Tha Phra Athit

BANGLAMPHU BARS

Banglamphu was once the
preserve of backpackers but
it now also attracts trendy
Thais. Thanon Khao San
has several café terraces
but the more interesting
bar scene is definitely on
nearby Soi Rambutri, with
everything from the hop-
ping Bangkok Bar to a VW
camper turned cocktail
bar. More highbrow cafés
are found on Thanon Phra
Athit, where Thai artists and
intellectuals gather.

RATCHADAMNOEN STADIUM

This is one of the main
venues for Muay Thai
(Thai Boxing), an exciting
sport which utilizes every
part of the body to fend
off an opponent.

🚹 D4 ✉ Thanon
Ratchadamnoen Nok
☎ 0 2281 4205 🕐 Mon,
Wed, Thu 6.30pm, Sun
5pm 🚇 Skytrain Phaya Thai
then taxi

SUPATRA RIVER HOUSE

www.supatrariverhouse.net
Good Thai food is served
in this beautiful teak
house with the option
of great views from the
open-air terrace overlooking the river.

🚹 B5 ✉ 266 Soi Wat
Rakhang, Thonburi ☎ 0 2411
0305 🕐 Daily 11.30am–2pm
and 5.30–11pm. Dinner show
Sat 🚢 Shuttle boat from Tha
Maharat

WAT PHO THAI TRADITIONAL MASSAGE SCHOOL

www.watpomassage.com
This excellent school
offers professional Thai
massage courses includ-
ing foot massage, spa
treatments and advanced
medical massage. The
school also has a center
offering good, inexpensive
massages by experienced
nonsmiling masseurs.

🚹 C6 ✉ Thanon Sanam
Chai ☎ 0 2662 3533
🕐 Daily 9–4 👐 Courses
from 1 to 5 weeks; massages
daily 8–5 🚢 Tha Tien

Restaurants

PRICES

Prices are approximate, based on a 3-course meal for one person.

$$$	more than 2,000B
$$	1,000B–2,000B
$	under 1,000B

CHOTE CHITR ($$)

www.chotechitr.ch

This tiny, family-run place serves excellent fare and is preferred by those who like to seek out those little culinary gems. Food is cooked to order.

✚ C5 ✉ 146 Prang Pu Thorn, Thanon Tanao (close to Democracy Monument) ☎ 0 2221 4082 🕐 Mon–Sat 12–9 🚤 Tha Phra Athit

DECK BY THE RIVER ($$)

www.arunresidence.com

Reservations are necessary at this idylic outdoor restaurant set on a deck by the Chao Phraya River and with views across to Wat Arun. Early evening is particularly popular as the sun sets.

✚ B5 ✉ 36–38 Soi Pratoo Nok Young, Thanon Maharat ☎ 0 2221 9158 🕐 Mon–Thu 11–10, Fri–Sun 11am–1am 🚤 Tha Thien

HEMLOCK ($–$$)

Small but charming, Hemlock is frequented by Thai artists and writers as well as those who work at the many nearby nongovernmental organizations. The menu is extensive, with excellent Thai dishes from all over the country.

✚ C4 ✉ Thanon Phra Athit 56, Banglamphu ☎ 0 2282 7507 🕐 Mon–Fri 4pm–midnight, Sat 5pm–midnight 🚤 Tha Phra Athit

MAY KAIDEE'S VEGETARIAN RESTAURANT ($)

www.maykaidee.com

Tucked away down a lane, parallel to but behind Thanon Tanao, this small but friendly place is worth seeking out for its inexpensive green curry, carrot salad, fried water spinach and other vegetarian delights. The best dessert is the black sticky rice with coconut milk, banana and mango.

✚ C5 ✉ 59 Thanon Tanao (near Thanon Khao San)

HIGH TEA

The Chinese claim that hot tea is the best way to cool down and to recover from the heat. English tea is something of an institution in Bangkok. The traditional place to take it is the Author's Lounge in the Mandarin Oriental Hotel (▷ 58, 112), but the grand lobbies of the Four Seasons (▷ 112), and the Shangri-La Hotel (▷ 112) and Peninsula (▷ 112) also offer teatime buffets accompanied by uplifting classical music. The Banyan Tree (▷ 112) serves high tea or a Thai tiffin box.

☎ 0 2629 4413 🕐 Daily 9am–10pm 🚤 Tha Phra Athit

PRAYA DINING ($$)

www.prayapalazzo.com

This restaurant is on the ground floor of a boutique hotel. Select from Thai and international cuisine. Book a table and they will send their boat across the river to fetch you.

✚ C4 ✉ 757/1 Somdej Prapinklao Soi 2, Bangyeekan ☎ 0 2883 2998 🕐 Daily lunch, dinner 🚤 Tha Phra Athi

SEVEN SPOONS ($)

www.sevenspoonsbkk.wordpress.com

Located in a restored Chinese shophouse, this is a minimalist gastrobar serving contemporary cuisine with a Mediterranean twist.

✚ D5 ✉ 22–24 Chakkrapatipong ☎ 0 2629 9214 🕐 Tue–Sat 11–3 and 6pm–1am, Sun 6pm–1am 🚤 Tha Phra Athit then tuk-tuk

SHEEPSHANK PUBLIC HOUSE ($–$$)

www.sheepshankpublichouse.com

Modern American cuisine is on the menu in this converted boat repair shop with great views of the river. Great prices, and not a burger in sight!

✚ C4 ✉ Thanon Phra Athit 47, Chana Songkram, Phra Nakhon ☎ 0 2629 5165 🕐 Tue–Sun 6pm–midnight 🚤 Tha Phra Athit

Bangkok's bustling business area has wholesalers in the alleys of Chinatown, and the towers of the major banks on Silom and Sathorn roads. In the middle of it all are temples, museums and sights.

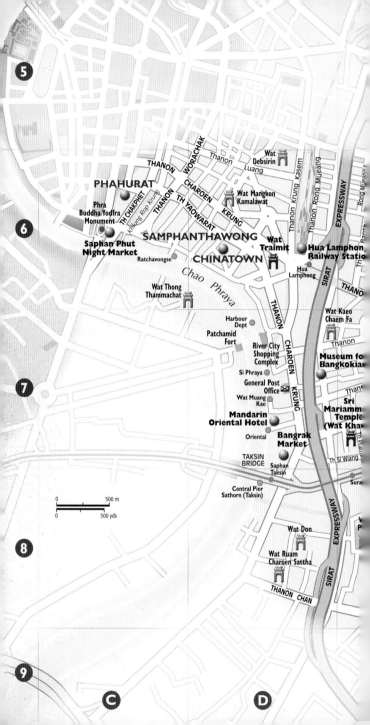

5

THANON

WORACHAK

Thanon
Luang

Wat
Debsirin

Thanon Krung Kasem

Thanon Rong Muang

Rong Muang

EXPRESSWAY

PHAHURAT

THANON

CHAROEN

TH CHAKPHET

TH YAOWARAT

Wat Mangkon
Kamalawat

Phra
Buddha Yodfra
Monument

Khlong Rop Krung

KRUNG

6

SAMPHANTHAWONG

**Wat
Traimit**

Hua Lamphon
Railway Statio

**Saphan Phut
Night Market**

Ratchavongse

CHINATOWN

Hua
Lamphong

SIRAT

THANO

Chao Phraya

Wat Thong
Thammachat

THANON

Wat Kaeo
Chaem Fa

Harbour
Dept

CHAROEN

Thanon

Patchamid
Fort

River City
Shopping
Complex

KRUNG

**Museum fo
Bangkokia**

7

Si Phraya

General Post
Office

Than

Wat Muang
Kae

**Sri
Mariamm
Temple
(Wat Kha**

**Mandarin
Oriental Hotel**

Oriental

**Bangrak
Market**

Th Si Wiang

TAKSIN
BRIDGE

Saphan
Taksin

Sura

Central Pier
Sathorn (Taksin)

0   500 m

0   500 yds

8

Wat Don

EXPRESSWAY

Wat Ruam
Charoen Sattha

SIRAT

THANON CHAN

9

C

D

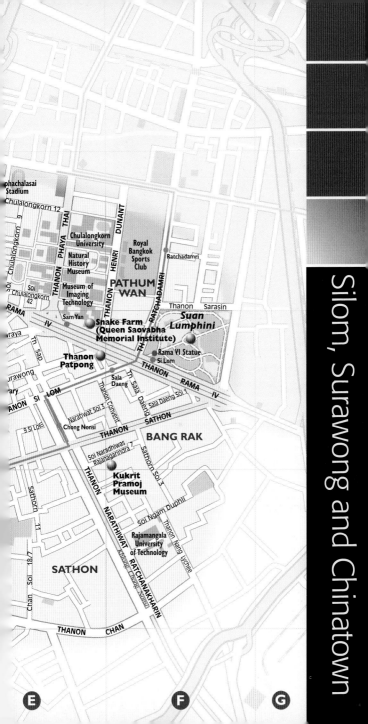

phachalasai
Stadium
Chulalongkorn 12

Chulalongkorn
University

Natural
History
Museum

THANON PHAYA THAI

THANON HENRI DUNANT

Museum of
Imaging
Technology

PATHUM
WAN

Royal
Bangkok
Sports
Club

Ratchadamri

THANON RATCHADAMRI

Chulalongkorn

Soi
Chulalongkorn
42

RAMA

araya

Th
Sap

Sam Yan

Snake Farm
(Queen Saovabha
Memorial Institute)

Thanon   Sarasin

Suan
Lumphini

IV

urawong

rary

SI LOM

THANON

Thanon
Patpong

9 Si LoEi

Th Sap

Sala
Daeng

Thanon Convent

Chong Nonsi

Narathiwat Soi 3

THANON

Sala Daeng

Sala Daeng Soi 1

THANON   RAMA   IV

SATHON

Rama VI Statue
Si Lom

Soi Naradhiwas
Rajanagarindra

7

THANON NARATHIWAT

Kukrit
Pramoj
Museum

BANG RAK

Sathon Soi 3

Soi Ngam Duphli

THANON RATCHANAKHARIN

Sathon

Rajamangala
University
of Technology

Thanon Nang Lychee

Khlong Chong Nonsi

Sathon 11

Chan Soi 18/7

SATHON

Chan Soi 3

THANON   CHAN

E

F

G

Chinatown

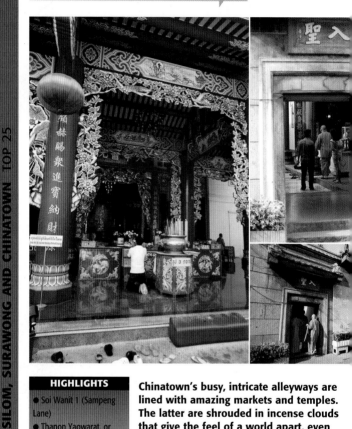

HIGHLIGHTS

● Soi Wanit 1 (Sampeng Lane)
● Thanon Yaowarat, or "Gold Street"
● Sala Chalermkrung Royal Theatre
● Wat Traimit (▷ 57)
● Nakorn Kasem (Thieves' Market)
● Soi Isaraphap
● Shanghai Inn

Chinatown's busy, intricate alleyways are lined with amazing markets and temples. The latter are shrouded in incense clouds that give the feel of a world apart, even in Bangkok.

The Chinese community By the 14th century Chinese merchants had set up vital trading centers in Thailand and were the only foreigners allowed to live within the walls of Ayutthaya. The Chinese were already well established in Bangkok when King Rama I built his capital on their grounds in 1782 and moved them to the Sampeng area. For a long time Chinatown was the city's commercial center, also gaining notoriety for its brothels, teahouses and opium dens. The restored Sala Chalermkrung Royal Theater (▷ 65)

Clockwise from far left: At the heart of Chinatown is the Chinese-Buddhist temple of Wat Mangkon Kamalawat; looking into the interior of Wat Mangkon Kamalawat; a busy market; the gateway that leads to Wat Mangkon Kamalawat; a specialty noodle maker prepares a dish; Buddhist monks entering a temple

is a perfect example of the theaters in the area. Chinese temples seem more down to earth than their Thai counterparts, one of the liveliest being Leng Noi Yee (▷ 60), which means "Dragon Lotus Temple." It has Buddhist, Taoist and Confucianist altars. You will find old Chinese men playing chess and watching the crocodiles in Wat Chakrawat.

Street markets Chinatown reveals its true soul in its street markets, old shophouses and shopping streets. The busiest alleyways are Soi Wanit 1 (Sampeng Lane) and Soi Isaraphap, and through the heart of it all cuts Thanon Yaowarat, famous for its gold shops. Nakorn Kasem, the so-called Thieves' Market, may no longer offer bargains but it is still great for a stroll and soaking up all the atmosphere.

THE BASICS

✚ C6–D6

🍴 Street stalls, food markets, White Orchid Hotel for excellent dim sum

🚇 Hua Lamphong

🚢 Tha Ratchawong pier

♿ Few

TIP

● The walk on page 60 minimizes the chances of losing your bearings amid the warren of small streets and narrow alleyways.

Suan Lumphini

HIGHLIGHTS

- Lumphini is Bangkok's biggest inner-city park.
- Chatuchak Park is near the weekend market (▷ 98).
- Pleasant Benjasiri Park is between Soi 22–25 on Thanon Sukhumvit (▷ 80).
- Small Santichaiprakan Park (▷ 42) is on Thanon Phra Sumen in Banglamphu and is popular with locals.

A small town in southern Nepal where the Buddha was born gives its name to this large park in downtown Bangkok. At first the park looks rather sad and dusty, but spend time in this pulsating city and the value of Lumphini becomes apparent.

An oasis of calm It is a vast expanse of green within the buzzing city—a place to seek some respite from the frenzy of urban stress and enjoy some moments of peace and quiet.

First light Lumphini is a place of moods rather than sights. In the early morning, before 7am, the park is full of people exercising. The graceful, Chinese-led t'ai chi groups make slow movements to music. At this hour traders also sell snake blood, a powerful tonic. Suddenly, all

Clockwise from far left: The view of the city from Lumphini Park; a shady spot by the boating lake; fountain displays; the park's open-air gym; the local reptiles like to bask in the sunshine, too

this activity comes to an abrupt halt and everyone stands to attention as the PA system plays the national anthem. By 9am, when the sun is up and rush-hour traffic has started, the crowd thins out.

Last light There's a different crowd in the afternoon. Joggers run on the 1.5-mile (2.5km) track, people pump weights at the open-air gym, and, in the windy season (February to April), kites soar above the busy city—at the height of the season you can buy beautiful kites here. When the light softens so does the atmosphere. Couples come out, foodstalls are set up and boats are rowed on the artificial lake until, at 6pm, with traffic at a halt in the evening rush, people in the park also stand still as the national anthem is played again.

THE BASICS

➕ F7

✉ Bordered by Thanon Rama IV, Thanon Ratchadamri, Thanon Witthaya (Wireless Road) and Thanon Sarasin

🕐 Daily 4.30am–9pm

🍴 Restaurant and food-stalls on the north side

🚇 Skytrain Sala Daeng

🚇 Lumphini and Silom

♿ Very good

🎟 Free

❓ The boating concession is open 5am–8pm. Avoid dogs at all costs; people in the park have been bitten by rabid dogs

Thanon Patpong

Street market (left); a band performs in Radio City café-bar (below)

THE BASICS

➕ E7

✉ Soi Patpong 1, 2, 3, 4, between Thanon Silom and Thanon Surawong

🕐 Most exciting after sunset until 1am

🍴 Many good restaurants and countless foodstalls

🚆 Skytrain Sala Daeng

Ⓜ Silom

♿ None

DID YOU KNOW?

● Seventy years ago Patpong was an undeveloped plot of land with just one teak house. After the Vietnam war it was bought for US$3,000 by Poon Pat Patpong, a Chinese man who wanted it for a family home. His eldest son, Udom, however, began to develop the area as a commercial venture without his father's permission. Udom persisted and today the area is worth many millions of US dollars, and literally billions of Thai Baht.

Patpong—two parallel streets and a lane running between Thanon Silom and Thanon Surawong—is renowned as a vibrant nightlife center, but also offers a busy night market, good bookstores and several restaurants.

The strip that never used to sleep The area is most busy in the evening. By day it's another Bangkok shopping street of bookstores, pharmacies and supermarkets. Late in the afternoon, foodstalls set up at either end of Patpong, some of them good enough to be reviewed in the city's English-language papers. Then bootleg DVDs and video games, cotton clothing, fake designer watches and souvenirs are laid out on Soi Patpong 1. Later the street fills with revelers.

Bars and restaurants Patpong is renowned for its go-go bars and discos. Despite its somewhat unsavory reputation, it's remarkably safe to visit—though it's as well to stick to the downstairs bars, as some of the upper-floor places have been known to overcharge. Patpong 1 has a few go-go bars but is mainly a shopping street where foreign couples shop and drink. Patpong 2 has numerous smaller beer bars (*ba bia* in Thai), as well as a row of karaoke establishments and some of the more popular restaurants on the strip. Patpong 3, an unassuming dead-end lane, is more of a gay venue. The strip comes alive in the early evening, but with the exception of a handful of places is more-or-less closed down by 1am.

Entrance (below); the Golden Buddha (middle); an outdoor shrine (right)

Wat Traimit

The Temple of the Golden Buddha is one of Bangkok's most popular places to visit. But no matter how many tourists crowd around, the Golden Buddha remains unruffled.

The Golden Buddha The shiny, 10ft (3m) tall gold Buddha, which weighs a hefty 7.4 tons, is believed to be the largest golden Buddha image in the world. The sculpture, made in Sukhothai in the 13th century, was covered with stucco as a disguise to protect it from the Burmese invaders of the 18th century. The disguise served the statue well as it wasn't until 1955, when workmen moved the Buddha image to a new building and spotted there was something shining through some cracks, that the stucco was taken off and the solid gold structure was revealed. The discovery sparked a national treasure hunt, but nothing else of similar value was found. It seems more than appropriate then that the Golden Buddha has found its home in Chinatown, which is, after all, at the center of Bangkok's gold trade. The statue is now valued at more than US$14 million, and several bits of stucco are on display to the left of it.

A less impressive temple The temple itself probably dates from the early 13th century. The statue of Reverend Phra Visutha-Thibordee, the abbot who ordered the construction of the new temple for the Golden Buddha, sits just opposite it and is covered in gold leaf.

THE BASICS

- D6
- Thanon Traimit, off Thanon Charoen Krung, Chinatown
- ☎ 0 2255 9775
- Daily 9–5
- Foodstalls in Chinatown
- Hua Lamphong
- None
- Inexpensive

DID YOU KNOW?

● Every Buddha image should be treated with respect.
● Some of Thailand's finest art was produced during the Sukhothai period (13th–15th centuries).
● Sukhothai Buddhas are usually seated with hands in the Bhumisparsa Mudra position, the right hand touching the earth and the left resting in the lap.

More to See

HUA LAMPHONG RAILWAY STATION

A superb example of Thai-style art deco, this beautiful central-hub railroad station was built in 1913 by Dutch architects.
✚ D6 ✉ Thanon Phra Rama IV
🚇 Hua Lamphong

KUKRIT PRAMOJ MUSEUM

www.kukritshousefund.com
The house of the former prime minister, M.R. Kukrit Pramoj, a great-grandson of King Rama II, who lived here until 1995, is one of the few places that gives an insight into traditional upper-class Thai life. Built in teak in Ayutthaya style, it has five beautiful rooms in a cluster. The interior is mostly as it was left in 1995. It includes modern air-conditioning, fine antiques and the *mai dat*, or Thai miniature trees, that were his passion.
✚ E8–F7 ✉ 19 Soi Phra Phinit (Soi 7), Thanon Narathiwat Ratchanakharun
☎ 0 2286 8185 🕐 Sat–Sun 10–5
🚉 Skytrain Chong Nonsi 💷 Inexpensive

MANDARIN ORIENTAL HOTEL

www.mandarinoriental.com
There are hotels, and then there's the Oriental. Nothing remains of the original 1876 Oriental, but the colonial Authors' Residence is the surviving building of 1887. This section contains the most luxurious suites, named after such illustrious guests as Noel Coward, and continues to attract celebrities. The lounge is a great place to enjoy afternoon tea. The luxurious spa offers every imaginable treat. There is also a world-class cookery school, and an excellent cultural program run by university professors.
✚ D7 ✉ 48 Soi Oriental ☎ 0 2659 9000 🍴 Restaurants and bar 🚉 Skytrain Saphan Taksin (free shuttle boat to hotel from Sathorn pier) ⛴ Tha Oriental pier ♿ Good
❓ Smart-casual dress. Residency not needed for spa or classes

MUSEUM FOR BANGKOKIANS

Ms Warapom Surawadi inherited this beautiful teak house and opened it as a folk museum. Call

View through the lush gardens, toward the old part of the Mandarin Oriental Hotel

Hua Lamphong Station

ahead so she can delight you with her stories (in English) of how she grew up in this house and how Thai people used to live. Her mother's first husband was a British-Indian doctor, and a separate house unit is devoted to him; her father was Chinese and her mother one of the first Thai women to go to university.
🚩 D7 ✉ 273 Soi Charoen Krung off Thanon Charoen Krung ☎ 0 2234 6741 🕐 Wed–Sun 10–4 (ring bell or call ahead)

PHAHURAT
Phahurat is Bangkok's Little India. Most of the shops sell fabrics, everything from silk to furnishing fabrics, and gems. Just off Thanon Chakraphet is Sri Gurusingh Sabha, a Sikh temple with golden domes. Every day at 9am blessed food is offered to devotees.
🚩 C6 🚢 Tha Saphan Phut pier

SAPHAN PHUT NIGHT MARKET
This market is popular with bargain hunters looking for secondhand clothing and those looking to have their portrait painted by one of the resident young artists.
🚩 C6 ✉ Memorial Bridge 🕐 Tue–Sun 8pm–1am 🚢 Tha Saphan Phut

SNAKE FARM (QUEEN SAOVABHA MEMORIAL INSTITUTE)
www.saovabha.com
Here you'll find a wide-ranging display of poisonous snakes, plus demonstrations of snake handling and venom milking.
🚩 E7 ✉ 1871 Rama IV ☎ 0 2252 0161 🕐 Mon–Fri 8.30–4, Sat, Sun 8.30–noon 🚇 Skytrain Sala Daeng 🚇 Sam Yan 👆 Moderate

SRI MARIAMMAN TEMPLE (WAT KHAEK)
Built during the 1860s, this Hindu temple is devoted to Uma Devi (Shakti) consort of Shiva, and her sons Kanthakumara and the elephant-headed Ganesh.
🚩 E7 ✉ Corner of Thanon Silom and Thanon Pan ☎ 0 2238 4007 🕐 Daily 6am–8pm 🚇 Skytrain Chong Nonsi

Snake-handling demonstration at Queen Saovabha Memorial Institute (Snake Farm)

Around Chinatown

Chinatown is busy, noisy and smelly, but nonetheless a sensory and cultural experience.

DISTANCE: 1.5 miles (2.5km) **ALLOW:** 3 hours

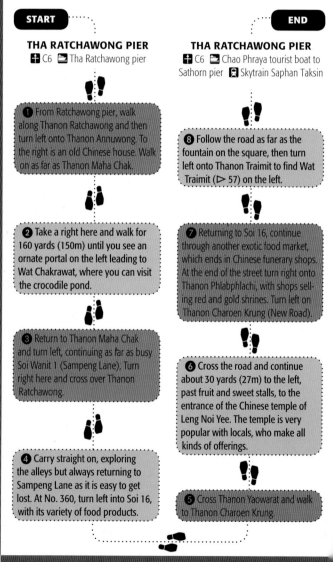

START

THA RATCHAWONG PIER
✚ C6 🚢 Tha Ratchawong pier

END

THA RATCHAWONG PIER
✚ C6 🚢 Chao Phraya tourist boat to Sathorn pier 🚊 Skytrain Saphan Taksin

❶ From Ratchawong pier, walk along Thanon Ratchawong and then turn left onto Thanon Annuwong. To the right is an old Chinese house. Walk on as far as Thanon Maha Chak.

❷ Take a right here and walk for 160 yards (150m) until you see an ornate portal on the left leading to Wat Chakrawat, where you can visit the crocodile pond.

❸ Return to Thanon Maha Chak and turn left, continuing as far as busy Soi Wanit 1 (Sampeng Lane). Turn right here and cross over Thanon Ratchawong.

❹ Carry straight on, exploring the alleys but always returning to Sampeng Lane as it is easy to get lost. At No. 360, turn left into Soi 16, with its variety of food products.

❽ Follow the road as far as the fountain on the square, then turn left onto Thanon Traimit to find Wat Traimit (▷ 57) on the left.

❼ Returning to Soi 16, continue through another exotic food market, which ends in Chinese funerary shops. At the end of the street turn right onto Thanon Phlabphlachi, with shops selling red and gold shrines. Turn left on Thanon Charoen Krung (New Road).

❻ Cross the road and continue about 30 yards (27m) to the left, past fruit and sweet stalls, to the entrance of the Chinese temple of Leng Noi Yee. The temple is very popular with locals, who make all kinds of offerings.

❺ Cross Thanon Yaowarat and walk to Thanon Charoen Krung.

Shopping

ANITA THAI SILK

www.anitasilk.com

Anita Thai Silk is recommended by expatriates as the place to find reasonably priced and good-quality silk. You'll find a wide selection of fabrics, plus men's shirts and neckties.

🞧 E7 ✉ 294/4–5 Thanon Silom ☎ 0 2234 2481 🚇 Skytrain Sala Daeng

A-PRIME CUSTOM TAILOR

www.a-primetailor.com

Men and women are catered to at this well-established and experienced tailor. Here you'll receive good personal service and high-quality work—if you don't need a suit in a day.

🞧 D7 ✉ Unit 101 Floor 1, Chao Phraya Tower, Soi 89 Wat Suan Plu ☎ 0 2630 6919 🚇 Skytrain Saphan Taksin

ART'S TAILORS

Unlike some other tailors in the city, Art's needs two to three weeks and several fittings to make a suit, but regulars insist that their creations are well worth the wait. This tailor's shop has an established reputation for excellent work.

🞧 E7 ✉ 62/15–16 Soi Thaniya, off Thanon Silom ☎ 0 2236 7966 🚇 Skytrain Sala Daeng

ASHWOOD GALLERY

This amazing antiques shop offers top-quality antique Chinese furniture and objets d'art. Prices are high, but then a lot of things are of excellent museum quality. You'll find another branch at the OP Place opposite the Mandarin Oriental (tel 0 2266 0187).

🞧 D7 ✉ Room 314 and 430, River City Shopping Complex, 23 Thanon Yotha ☎ 0 2237 0077, ext. 314 or 430 ⛴ Tha Sri Phraya pier

ASIA BOOKS

www.asiabooks.com

This is Thailand's premier bookstore with a great selection of English-language books and books on Thailand and all of its regions beyond Bangkok.

🞧 E7 ✉ 3rd floor, Thaniya Plaza Building on Thanon Thaniya, off Thanon Silom ☎ 0 2231 2106-7 🚇 Skytrain Sala Daeng Ⓜ Silom

BOOKAZINE

This chain is owned by the biggest foreign magazine publisher in Thailand, so the selection of foreign publications is excellent. Good English-language selection and loads of books on Thailand and Southeast Asia.

🞧 E7 ✉ Silom Complex (2nd Floor), corner of Thanon Silom and Rama IV ☎ 0 2231 3135, ext. 301 🚇 Skytrain Sala Daeng Ⓜ Silom

H GALLERY

www.hgallerybkk.com

Some of the most trend-setting contemporary Thai art for sale in the city can be bought at this gallery in a beautiful old house.

🞧 E7 ✉ 201 Sathorn Soi 12 ☎ 085 021 5508 🚇 Skytrain Chong Nonsi

JAANA

www.jaanagallery.com

This small jewelry store has some amazing unique necklaces and other jewelry, using semi-precious stones, amulets and silver from Thailand, but also picked up on the designer's travels.

🞧 D7 ✉ Room 246, River City Shopping Complex, 23 Thanon Yotha ☎ 0 2639 6044 ⛴ Tha Sri Phraya pier

TAILOR-MADE CLOTHES

Bangkok tailors, mostly Thais of Indian origin, have taken over from their Hong Kong brothers. It is cheaper to have a suit made than to buy a designer suit, but remember that you get what you pay for. Some tailors offer a package of two suits, jacket, kimono and shirts, all made in 24 hours for little over 4,300B, but the quality will be nonexistent. Choose a tailor with a good reputation, choose a quality fabric and good cut and allow the tailor as much time as possible. You will need to go to the shop to choose your fabric, but fittings can usually be done in your hotel room.

JIM THOMPSON FACTORY OUTLET STORE

This factory outlet offers an excellent choice of quality furnishing fabrics at bargain prices. There is another factory outlet at 153 Sukhumvit 93 (▷ 87).

⊞ E7 ✉ 149/4-6 Thanon Surawong ☎ 0 2235 8930–2 🚇 Skytrain Sala Daeng

JIM THOMPSON'S THAI SILK COMPANY

www.jimthompson.com
This is the best, but not the cheapest, place to buy silks and a range of silk clothing. The quality and the variety of colors and textures is superior to most other shops selling this delicate fabric. Don't miss the excellent furnishing fabrics, both cotton and silk. Also good, top-priced silk shirts and neckties are on sale, in a wide, though conservative, range of patterns and colors, as well as jackets, pajamas and robes. There are branches of this store in most five-star hotels and at the Emporium Shopping Complex (▷ 86).

⊞ E7 ✉ 9 Thanon Surawong ☎ 0 2632 8100 🚇 Skytrain Sala Daeng

JOHNY'S GEMS

www.johnysgems.com
Johny's Gems is one of the city's oldest jewelry emporiums. Choose from a selection of jewelry to suit all budgets.

⊞ D6 ✉ 199 Thanon Fueng Nakorn, Chinatown ☎ 0 2224 4065 📞 Phone for free shuttle from your hotel

LAMBERT INDUSTRIES LTD

www.lambertgems.com
Lambert Industries has a respected reputation and has been offering gem-cutting services, ready-to-wear jewelry and gemstones for almost four decades. They make bespoke creations for clients all across the world.

⊞ E7 ✉ 807–809 Silom Shanghai Building, 4th Floor, Soi 17, Silom Road ☎ 0 2236 4343 🚇 Skytrain Surasak

THAI ANTIQUES

Fakes are particularly well made in Thailand and are sometimes sold as genuine antiques. To protect yourself, buy from a reputable shop. Antiques and Buddha images cannot be exported without a license, which can be obtained from the Fine Arts Department at the National Museum (Thanon Naphratad, tel 0 2221 4817). Some antiques stores will arrange the paperwork for you. Applications, submitted with two photographs of the object and a photocopy of your passport, usually take about five days to be processed.

LIN SILVERCRAFT

www.lynjewelers.com
Specialties of this silver shop include cuff links engraved to order, silver necklaces, bangles and cutlery. It is not the cheapest shop in town but the quality is good.

⊞ D7 ✉ 3 & 9 Thanon Charoen Krung, 50138 ☎ 0 2234 2819/2391 🚇 Skytrain Saphan Taksin

LOFT

www.loftbangkok.com
Choose from stationery to homeware and laptop and mobile phone accessories to bags, purses and rucksacks at this branch of the stylish chain.

⊞ E6 ✉ Siam Discovery (4th–5th Floor), 989 Rama 1 Road ☎ 0 2658 0328 🚇 Skytrain Sala Daeng

NEOLD

This wonderful shop, owned by one of Thailand's top antiques dealers and designers, specializes in combining the new with the old. High-quality antiques, baskets, lacquerware, tapestries and furniture. There is another branch at the Four Seasons Hotel (▷ 112).

⊞ E7 ✉ 149/2–3 Thanon Surawong ☎ 0 2239 8919 🚇 Skytrain Sala Daeng

OLD MAPS AND PRINTS

www.classicmaps.com
Browse here among old maps of Siam and South Asia, or look for fine

prints. The knowledgeable owner, Joerg Kohler, can tell you all about them.

➕ D7 ✉ 432 River City Shopping Complex, 23 Thanon Yotha, off Thanon Sri Phraya ☎ 0 2237 0077, ext. 432 🚢 Tha Sri Phraya pier

PATPONG NIGHT BAZAAR

Bangkok's famous red-light area is also the site for a very popular night market. The sidewalks of Patpong 1 and nearby Thanon Silom fill with stands displaying clothes with counterfeit designer labels, counterfeit Rolex watches, bootleg music and movies, leatherware, and other merchandise.

➕ E7 ✉ Patpong 1 🕐 Nightly 6pm–late 🚇 Silom 🚉 Skytrain Sala Daeng

RIVER CITY SHOPPING COMPLEX

This four-story mall over-looks the Chao Phraya River. It specializes in antiques and collectibles but also offers a good selection of fashion outlets as well as riverside restaurants.

➕ D7 ✉ Charoen Krung Soi 30 (next to Royal Orchid Sheraton Hotel) ☎ 0 2237 0077 🚉 Skytrain Saphan Taksin 🚤 River City Shuttle Boat

SIAM BRONZE FACTORY

www.siambronze.com
Siam Bronze specializes in the highest quality bronze and stainless steel products. Its trademark is cutlery, dining utensils and homeware, and it will ship worldwide.

➕ D8 ✉ 1250 New Road, Bangkok ☎ 0 2234 9436 🕐 Call for appointment 🚉 Skytrain Saphan Taksin

SILOM VILLAGE

www.silomvillage.co.th
Silom Village is the most visitor-oriented attraction on Thanon Silom. There is a series of several shopping malls, a hotel, spa, the Ruen Thep Thai Dance Center and restaurants. The outlets mostly sell handicrafts and

jewelry, but there is also a clothes boutique, luggage shops and a tailor's shop. Prices are quite steep so you need to bargain.

➕ E7 ✉ 286 Thanon Silom ☎ 0 2234 4448 🚉 Skytrain Chong Nonsi

TABTIM DREAMS COMPANY

Tabtim has specialized in rubies, sapphires and one of a kind jewelry pieces for almost 30 years.

➕ E7 ✉ 919/1 Jewelry Trade Center, JTC Building, Unit 108 Bangrak ☎ 0 2630 0815 🚉 Skytrain Surasak 🚢 Tha Oriental pier

THAI HOME INDUSTRIES

Shelves heave with baskets, cotton farmers' clothes, temple bells, pretty glass lamps, and settings of the company's stylish, bronze and metal cutlery at this shop set in a dusty teak house.

➕ D7 ✉ 35 Soi Oriental ☎ 0 2234 1736 🚢 Tha Oriental pier

THE FINE ARTS

A beautiful store selling miniature wooden boats, amulets, 19th-century silks and costumes. Also for sale are textiles from Southeast Asia, collected by the owner.

➕ D7 ✉ Rooms 354 and 452–4, River City Shopping Complex, 23 Thanon Yotha, off Thanon Sri Phraya ☎ 0 2237 0077, ext. 354/452/554 🚢 Tha Sri Phraya pier

Entertainment and Nightlife

70S BAR

1970s glam is the order of the day in this happening place—especially with the gay crowd. Hits from the decade blend with Thai pop and hip-hop on the upper level, while downstairs are a street-level bar and lounge.

✚ F6 ✉ 231/16 Sarasin, behind Lumphini Park ☎ 0 2253 4433 🚆 Skytrain Ratchadamri

ALLIANCE FRANÇAISE

www.afthailand.org
The Alliance is very active, offering a busy program of French movies, concerts and lectures.

✚ F7 ✉ 29 Thanon Satorn Tai ☎ 0 2670 4200 🚆 Skytrain Chong Nonsi

BAMBOO BAR

A tastefully decorated and homey bar with a barman who knows how to handle his shaker. After 10pm there are live jazz bands, often from the US.

✚ D7 ✉ Mandarin Oriental Hotel, 48 Soi Oriental ☎ 0 2659 9000 🕐 Sun–Thu 11am–1am, Fri, Sat 11am–2am 🚆 Skytrain Saphan Taksin ⛴ Tha Oriental pier

BANYAN TREE SPA

www.banyantreespa.com
Enjoy the fantastic views over the city as you relax in this elegant spa. Massages come in all kinds: Swedish, Balinese and traditional Thai. Spa weekends for couples are on offer.

✚ F7 ✉ Thai Wah II Building, 21/100 Thanon Sathon Tai ☎ 0 2679 1052 🚇 Lumphini

THE BARBICAN

This popular British pub sometimes has live music, but often has DJs playing the latest tunes. Good tapas and other international cuisine.

✚ E7 ✉ 9/4–5 Soi Thaniya, off Thanon Silom ☎ 0 2234 3590 🕐 Daily 11.30am–1am 🚆 Skytrain Sala Daeng 🚇 Silom

BENJARONG ROYAL THAI CUISINE COOKERY CLASSES

www.lecordonbleudusit.com
It's one of the world's great cuisines, so why not pick up a trick or two at these half-day cookery classes run by the restaurant's head chef.

✚ F7 ✉ Dusit Thani Hotel, 946 Rama IV Road ☎ 0 2200 9000, ext. 2699 🕐 Mon–Fri

> ### ADMISSION CHARGES
>
> Many discos have a cover charge, which usually includes one or two drinks. These charges are often doubled on Friday and Saturday evenings, but that's when the fun is to be had (discos tend to be quite dull during week-days). Many clubs refuse entry to men in shorts and sandals and prefer smart-casual dress.

2pm–5pm 💷 3,000B–4,200B (includes set dinner in the restaurant) 🚆 Skytrain Sala Daeng 🚇 Silom

DISTIL & SKY BAR

www.thedomebkk.com
The lounge and cigar bar on the 64th floor of the State Tower, offers spectacular views and luxurious nibbles. This bar has been used as a movie location, namely *The Hangover II*.

✚ D7 ✉ State Tower, 1055 Thanon Silom ☎ 0 2624 9555 🕐 Daily 6pm–1am 🚇 Saphan Taksin

GOETHE INSTITUT

www.goethe.de/bangkok
A cultural venue for films, lectures and concerts.

✚ F7 ✉ 18/1 Soi Goethe, Sathon 1 ☎ 0 2108 8200 🕐 Telephone for schedule 🚇 Lumphini

JOE LOUIS PUPPET THEATRE

www.joelouistheatre.com
Come here to see the disappearing art of the traditional Hun Lakorn Lek Thai puppets.

✚ D7 ✉ Asiatique The Riverfront, 2194 Thanon Charoen Krung Road ☎ 0 2688 3322/0909 🕐 Shows daily at 7.30pm 🚆 Skytrain Saphan Taksin

KITE-FLYING

Kite-flying is a national pastime in Thailand and not confined to children. Contests between rival teams can be serious affairs. In Lumphini

Park and Sanam Luang, however, the emphasis is on fun. Vendors sell ingeniously designed kites around both parks.
🚩 F7, B–C5 ☒ Lumphini Park and Sanam Luang 🕐 Daily Feb–Apr, daytime 🚇 Silom or Lumphini (Lumphini Park) 🚌 Sala Daeng (Lumphini Park); Phaya Thai and then a taxi (Sanam Luang) 🚢 Tha Phra Chan pier (Sanam Luang)

LUMPHINI BOXING STADIUM
www.muaythailumpinee. net/en
This venue showcases the popular sport of *muay thai* (Thai boxing). Expect some bloodshed.
🚩 F7 ☒ Thanon Rama IV, near Lumphini Park ☎ 0 2251 4303 🕐 Tue and Fri at 6.30pm, Sat at 4pm and 9pm 🚇 Lumphini

NORIEGA'S
Live blues and jazz bands perform here nightly, and there is an open-mic night on Wednesdays.
🚩 F7 ☒ Silom Soi 4 ☎ 0 2233 2813 🕐 Daily 4pm–1am 🚌 Skytrain Sala Daeng 🚇 Silom

RUEN-NUAD MASSAGE STUDIO
A real find, this massage studio in a delightful teak house offers Thai or aromatic oil massages.
🚩 E–F7 ☒ 42 Thanon Convent, Silom ☎ 0 2632 2662 🕐 Daily 10–9, but call ahead to reserve 🚌 Skytrain Sala Daeng

SALA CHALERMKRUNG ROYAL THEATRE
www.salachalermkrung.com
The perfect place to see *knon* (traditional Thai masked dance drama).
🚩 D6 ☒ Thanon Charoen Krung, near crossroads with Thanon Tripetch ☎ 0 2222 0434 🚢 Tha Saphan Phut

SALA RIM NAAM
www.mandarinoriental.com/ bangkok
The Mandarin Oriental's Thai restaurant (▷ 58) is in a teak house beside the Chao Phraya River and offers a set menu dinner accompanied by classical Thai dancing.
🚩 D7 ☒ Mandarin Oriental, 48, Soi Oriental ☎ 0 2437 6211 🕐 Dinner from 7pm, dance from 8.30pm 🚌 Saphan Taksin 🚢 Tha Oriental pier

THAI BOXING TRAINING
Learn about Muay Thai at Muay Thai Institute (☒ 336/932 Prahonyothin 118 Thanon Vipravadee, Prachatipat, Thanyaburi, Pathum Thani ☎ 0 2992 0096/7, www.muaythai-institute.net) which specializes in training foreigners and Thai beginners. Instruction is given on boxing, refereeing, training and first aid, as well as the history and development of the sport. Accommodations are available.

THREE SIXTY
It's a grown-up crowd that's drawn to this stylish 32nd-floor venue across the Chao Phraya. The setting is circular and is also decidedly futuristic in design. The jazz is world class, the cocktail list impressive and the ambience seductive.
🚩 C7 ☒ Millennium Hilton Hotel, 123 Thanon Charoen Nakorn ☎ 0 2442 2000 🕐 Daily 5pm–1am 🚌 Saphan Taksin and hotel courtesy boat

VERTIGO
www.banyantree.com/bangkok
From 61 floors up the views are seriously impressive in this chic watering hole. It's a great place for a relaxing aperitif while night falls. Reservations are needed for the adjacent grill and restaurant (▷ 68).
🚩 F7 ☒ Banyan Tree Hotel, 21/100 Thanon South Sathorn ☎ 0 2679 1200 🕐 Daily 5pm–1am (weather permitting) 🚌 Sala Daeng 🚇 Lumphini

WET DECK
www.whotels.com/bangkok
This trendy outdoor space is a great place to bask in the sun and soak up local culture while sipping on customized cocktails and sampling the menu at The Kitchen Table, the hotel's modern bistro.
🚩 E7 ☒ 106 North Sathorn Road, Silom ☎ 0 2344 4401 🕐 Daily 10–10 🚌 Skytrain Chong Nonsi

Restaurants

PRICES

Prices are approximate, based on a 3-course meal for one person.

$$$	more than 2,000B
$$	1,000B–2,000B
$	under 1,000B

AUBERGINE ($$)

www.aubergine.in.th
Trademark French dishes are served in this attractive house on a quiet *soi* off Silom Road. The lamb rack is a favorite, the atmosphere is a blend of classy and cozy and the wine list is impressive.
🚹 E7 ✉ 71/1 Sala Daeng Soi 1/1 ☎ 0 2234 2226 🕐 Daily 11.30am–2.30pm, 6pm–11.30pm 🚇 Sala Daeng

BAAN KHANITHA ($$)

www.baan-khanitha.com
This huge, popular restaurant has a garden area and is a perfect introduction to Thai cuisine, as the dishes here have been adapted to the Western palate.
🚹 E8 ✉ 69 South Sathorn Road. Other branches at Sukhumvit 23 and 53, and at Asiatique ☎ 0 2675 4200 🕐 Lunch, dinner 🚇 Lumphini

BLUE ELEPHANT ($$$)

www.blueelephant.com/bangkok
The Blue Elephant made its name outside Thailand as a chain of gourmet Thai restaurants. The restaurant and cooking school is in a gorgeous colonial building. The menu offers a good mix of traditional royal cuisine, "Forgotten Recipes" and innovative Thai cuisine—"Our Chef's Creations."
🚹 E8 ✉ Blue Elephant Building, 233 South Sathorn Road ☎ 0 2673 9353 🕐 Daily 11.30am–2.30pm, 6.30–10.30 🚇 Skytrain Surasak

LE CAFÉ SIAM ($$)

An elegant restaurant in a charming house, where all the art and furniture is also for sale. The Michelin-starred food is half Thai, half French.
🚹 Off map ✉ 4 Soi Sriakson, off Thanon Chuea Phloeng, off Thanon Rama IV ☎ 0 2671 0030 🕐 Lunch, dinner 🚇 Khlong Toci

CHINESE CUISINE

If you want to cool your palate down after the often fiery Thai food, try one of the more authentic Chinese restaurants. Most Chinese in Bangkok come from the Guangdong and Yunnan provinces, well-known for their delicious cuisine. Some of the best food can be sampled at the hundreds of inexpensive street stalls in Chinatown, or in the more expensive Chinese restaurants in hotels—there are very few Chinese restaurants in the middle price range.

THE CAPITAL BY WATER LIBRARY ($$–$$$)

www.waterlibrary.com
Describing itself as "a quaint steakhouse-cum-seafood restaurant", The Capital by Water Library offers a quality meat selection from around the world, daily delivered seafood, and an eclectic range of wines, martinis and craft beers.
🚹 E7 ✉ Level 3, Empire Tower, South Sathorn Road, Silom ☎ 0 2286 9548 🕐 Mon–Sat 11.30am–midnight (kitchen closes at 11pm) 🚇 Skytrain Chong Nonsi

CELADON ($$–$$$)

www.sukhothai.com
One of Bangkok's most celebrated and beautiful restaurants. Inside it's minimalist Thai, outside there are lotus ponds and banana trees. The modern cuisine is just as wonderful; the roast duck curry is particularly good.
🚹 F7 ✉ Sukhothai Hotel, 13/3 South Sathorn Road ☎ 0 2344 8888 🕐 Lunch, dinner 🚇 Skytrain Sala Daeng

EAT ME ($$)

www.eatmerestaurant.com
Eat Me is an exciting restaurant set over several floors with terraces. The look is modern Asian, the music is great, waiters are friendly and the food is excellent. The menu changes but favorites remain, such as crab and

pomelo salad, linguine with spicy soft shell crab and sticky date pudding with hot butterscotch.
E7–F7 ✉ Soi Pipat 2, off Thanon Convent, Silom ☎ 0 2238 0931 🕐 3pm–1am 🚇 Skytrain Sala Daeng

HARMONIQUE ($–$$)
Old Chinese shophouse filled with antiques and fountains. Popular for its excellent Thai dishes.
D7 ✉ 22 Soi Charoen Krung 34 ☎ 0 2237 8175 🕐 Mon–Sat 11am–10pm 🚢 Tha Oriental

HORIZON RIVER CRUISE ($$)
These regular night cruises on the Chao Phraya include an international buffet with fresh salads, broiled fish, meats and very good desserts.
D7 ✉ Shangri-La Hotel, 89 Soi Wat Sun Plu, Bangrak ☎ 0 2236 9952 🚇 Skytrain Saphan Taksin 🚢 Tha Shangri-La pier

LORD JIM ($$$)
This is a superb and incredibly swish fish and seafood restaurant in an elegant setting overlooking the river. Impeccable service and tiny but wonderful little treats between courses, like a smoking sorbet or a pretty amuse-bouche.
D7 ✉ Top floor of Mandarin Oriental Hotel, 48 Soi Oriental ☎ 0 2659 9000 🕐 Lunch, dinner 🚇 Skytrain Saphan Taksin 🚢 Tha Oriental pier

LOY NAVA ($$–$$$)
www.loynava.com
Dinner is served on this enchanting teak rice barge full of charm and history. Elegant Thai dancers and musicians add to the atmosphere.
D7 ✉ Tha Oriental pier ☎ 0 2437 7329/4932 🕐 Departs 6pm and 8pm 🚢 Tha Oriental pier

LE LYS ($$)
www.lelys.info
A French-Thai couple runs this comfortable place. You can be sure of getting good Thai food.
E7 ✉ 148/11 Nang Linchi Soi 6, Thung Mahamek Sathorn ☎ 0 2287 1898/9 🕐 Daily noon–10.30pm 🚇 Skytrain Chong Nonsi

---

VEGETARIAN OPTIONS

Vegetarians who are visiting Bangkok during the annual Vegetarian Festival (September to October) will find Chinatown awash with foodstalls serving Thai and Chinese vegetarian dishes. At other times of the year a choice of fresh vegetable dishes is offered at most Indian and Thai restaurants. Most dishes can be made vegetarian, just mention you are *tann jay*. The city's best vegetarian restaurant is The Whole Earth (✉ 93/3 Soi Lang Suan, off Thanon Ploenchit ☎ 0 2252 5574).

MANGO TREE ($$)
www.coca.co.th/mangotree
A charming courtyard setting, attentive service and a superb menu of Thai favorites and delicacies make this a popular choice with locals and tourists. Booking advised on weekends.
E7 ✉ 37 Soi Tantawan, Thanon Surawongse ☎ 0 2236 2820 🕐 Daily 11am–midnight 🚇 Chong Nonsi

MEI JIANG ($$$)
www.bangkok-peninsula.com
Superb Cantonese dishes are served at this stunning Chinese restaurant that's decorated in an art deco style. Great views.
D7 ✉ Peninsula Hotel, 333 Thanon Charoen Nakorn ☎ 0 2861 2888 🕐 Lunch, dinner 🚇 Skytrain Saphan Taksin (shuttle boat to hotel)

NAHM ($$$)
www.comohotels.com/
metropolitanbangkok
Nahm delivers complex and authentic Thai delicacies from award-winning chef David Thompson in a dining room of chic elegance and sophistication. Standout dishes feature rare ingredients from across Thailand, including a jungle curry with *pla chorn* (a Thai freshwater fish) as well as salty and sweet Thai desserts.
F7 ✉ Metropolitan Hotel, 27 South Sathorn Road ☎ 0 2625 3333 🕐 Lunch, dinner 🚇 Skytrain Chong Nonsi 🚇 Lumphini

LE NORMANDIE ($$$)

For a formal, elegant dining experience, come to Le Normandie (you'll need to make a reservation). You'll find a choice of exquisite dishes prepared by Michelin-starred chefs, impeccable service and stunning views.

➕ D7 ✉ Top floor, Mandarin Oriental Hotel, 48 Soi Oriental ☎ 0 2659 9000 🕐 Lunch, dinner 🚊 Skytrain Saphan Taksin 🚢 Tha Oriental pier

PIERSIDE SEAFOOD RESTAURANT ($$)

Choose from the fresh seafood counter or order from the menu, which includes great crab in yellow curry and butter-baked Phuket lobsters. At night enjoy river views from the terrace or dine inside among lots of teak wood and gold leaf.

➕ D7 ✉ Ground level, River City Shopping Complex, 23 Soi Captain Bush ☎ 0 2639 4751/2 🕐 Lunch, dinner 🚢 Tha River City pier

RUEN URAI ($$)

www.ruen-urai.com
Don't be put off by the crowds around the notorious Patpong. This delightful eatery is tucked away in a century-old manor house where the emphasis is on traditional Thai tastes.

➕ E7 ✉ The Rose Hotel, 118 Thanon Surawongse ☎ 0 2266 8268 🕐 Daily noon–11pm 🚊 Skytrain Chong Nonsi

SALADAENG CAFÉ ($$)

Surrounded by sky-scrapers, this is a lovely converted house with a warm wood-paneled decor and outside tables. It serves good Thai food.

➕ F7 ✉ 120/1 Thanon Sala Daeng 1 ☎ 0 2266 9167 🕐 Lunch, dinner 🚊 Skytrain Sala Daeng 🚇 Lumphini

SALATHIP ($$$)

Come here for delightful Royal Thai cuisine in the elegant setting of a carved teak pavilion looking out over the Chao Phraya River.

➕ D7 ✉ Shangri-La Hotel, 8 Soi Wat Suan Phu ☎ 0 2236 7777 🕐 Daily 6.30pm–10.30pm 🚊 Skytrain Saphan

A TYPICAL THAI MEAL

Since the majority of Thais eat at street food stalls or at home, Thai restaurants in Bangkok are more oriented toward foreign visitors who may be unused to chilies. If you want your food red hot, mention it when you order otherwise you will be disappointed. A meal may consist of some appetizers or a spicy salad followed by at least one curry, a noodle dish, steamed rice and a soup. Thais eat with a spoon (right hand) and a fork (left hand). They take just one mouthful of a dish on their plate, then move to the next dish.

Taksin 🚢 Tha Oriental or Shangri-La piers

SILOM VILLAGE ($$)

www.silomvillage.co.th
Choose from a selection of fresh seafood and other Thai dishes at this huge semi-outdoor restaurant surrounded by craft and textile stores. There is traditional Thai dancing every night.

➕ E7 ✉ 286 Thanon Silom ☎ 0 2234 4448 🕐 Daily 10am–11pm 🚊 Skytrain Chong Nonsi

SWEET BASIL ($$)

Exquisite Vietnamese/Thai cuisine served in an old house in this quiet alley oozing with the atmosphere of an older Bangkok.

➕ E7 ✉ Thanon Sirivieng, off Soi Pramuan, Silom ☎ 0 2238 3088 🕐 Lunch, dinner 🚊 Skytrain Surasak

VERTIGO ($$–$$$)

www.banyantree.com/bangkok
Perched on the roof of the Banyan Tree Hotel, this sky bar has superb views over the city. The chic open-air lounge (▷ 65) is a wonderful spot at sunset. The restaurant serves excellent barbecued seafood and Asian fusion dishes. Reservations are needed.

➕ F7 ✉ 21/100 South Sathorn Road ☎ 0 2679 1200 🕐 Daily 6pm–11pm (weather permitting) 🚇 Lumphini 🚊 Skytrain Chong Nonsi

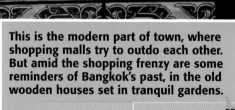

This is the modern part of town, where shopping malls try to outdo each other. But amid the shopping frenzy are some reminders of Bangkok's past, in the old wooden houses set in tranquil gardens.

Museum of
Floral Culture

DUSIT

SAMSEN

Thanon

Amnuay

Ratchasima

Phichai

Songkhram

Prem

Pracharkon

RAMA V

Sukhothai
Palace

THANON

Khlong

Nakhon

Nakhon

Samsen

Chaisi

Thanon

Thanon

Wat Noi
Nappakun

Thanon Set Siri

THANON

Sam Sen

Th Nakhon Chaisi

Church of the
Immaculate
Conception

Wat
Rachathiwat

Th Khao

THANON

Sukhothai

SAMSEN

Wat Sukhan
Tharam

Th Sukhothai

Wat Jom
Sudaram

Phet 5

Kamphaeng

Phra Thi Nang
Vimanmek

National
Library

Thewes

RAMA VIII
BRIDGE

Bank of
Thailand

THANON

Krung

Kasem

Thanon

Nakhon

Luk

Parliament
House

RATCHAWITHI

RAMA

Abhisek Dusit
Throne Hall

Anata
Samakhom
Throne Hall

Royal
Elephant Museum

Dusit
Zoo

Chitralada
Villa

THANON

RATCHAWITHI

Soi
Setsiri

Thanon

Yot

King Rama V
(Chulalongkorn)
Statue

SI

AYUTTHAYA

Sawankhalok

THANON

RATCHATHEW

Wat
Benchamabophit

Government
House

Wat
Sommanat

PHITSANULOK

Royal Turf Club

THANON

EXPRESSWAY

THANON

Phaya Thai

TH NAKHON SAWAN

THANON

LAN

LUANG

Th Damrongrak

Mahanak
Market

POM PRAP
SATTRU PHAI

Kanchanawanit
Market

Khlong

TH RAMA VI

SIRAT

Saen

TH PHAYA

THANON

PHAYA

Ratchathewi

Rong Liang
Dek Market

Thanon

Rama

Wat
Chai

Thanon Banthat Thong

Saen

Saep

Petchaburi
Market

Siam Discovery
Centre &
Madame
Tussauds

Baan Jim
Thompson

Si
Oce
Wo

TH RAMA I

National Stadium

Siam

MBK Center
(Mahboonkrong)

Siam

0   500 m

0   500 yds

3

4

5

6

7

C

D

E

Victory
Monument

SIRAT
EXPRESSWAY

Sol Attha Wimon

Sol Bun Yu

Victory
Monument

THANON

Phayathai
Market

DIN

Wat Thatsanarun
Suntrikaram

Thanon Rang Nam

Si Din Daeng
Market

DAENG

RATCHAPRAROP

Bangkok
Doll Factory

Fatima
Church

Wang Suan
Pakkad

AYUTTHAYA

Baiyoke
Tower II

Ratchaprarop

THANON

Makkasan

Makkasan
(Airport Link)

Don
Bosco

Phetchaburi

PETCHABURI

Pratunam
Market

antip
Plaza

Nai Lert
Park Shrine

TH CHIT LOM

TH WITTHAYU

CHALOEM

Sukhumvit 3 (Sol Nana Nua)

Sukhumvit Sol 15

Sol 13

Sol 11

THANON ASOK MONTRI

Central
World
Plaza

Narayana
Phand

Sol
Somkid

Gaysorn

PHLOEN

Central
Chidlom

THANON

Saan Phra
Phrom
(Erawan
Shrine)

Chit Lom

CHIT

Nana

THANON

Baan Kam
Thieng

Peninsula
Plaza

Thanon Lang Suan

Sol Ton Son

Sol Ruam Rudi

Phloen
Chit

MAHANAKHON

Sukhumvit 2

Thanon Duang

Thanon Sukhumvit

Sukhumvit 10

Asok

Sukhumvit

THANON

Sukhumvit Sol 18

SUKHUMVIT

WITTHAYU

THANON

EXPRESSWAY

Thanon Phithak

Calvary
Baptist
Church

Benjakiti
Park

RATCHADAPHISEK

Sukhumvit Sol 16

Lumphini

Lumphini
Boxing
Stadium

F

G

H

Abhisek Dusit Throne Hall

Views inside and outside the throne hall, with its exquisite latticework

The Abhisek Dusit Throne Hall, built in a harmonious Euro-Thai-Moorish style, has a display of handicrafts, such as *mutmee* silk, nielloware and basketry, made by Queen Sirikit's SUPPORT Foundation.

A concoction of styles Just east of the Vimanmek Palace (▷ 77) is this unusual pavilion, built as a throne hall by King Rama V in 1904. Although clearly influenced by the architectural style of Victorian mansions and Moorish follies, the charming one-story building also shows a distinctive Thai character. The Throne Hall was only ever used to receive the foreign ambassadors visiting the Dusit Palace. The building overlooks the immaculate European-style lawns and flowerbeds.

The Queen Sirikit SUPPORT Foundation The throne hall, with its elaborate interior, was restored and reopened by the current king and queen in 1993. It now houses a display of arts and crafts produced in rural communities under the patronage of the queen's Foundation for the Promotion of Supplementary Occupation and Related Techniques (SUPPORT). This acclaimed project has allowed impoverished farmers to earn some extra cash, but equally importantly, it has helped to revive certain near-extinct traditional crafts. Displays include fine nielloware, handmade gold- and silverware, colorful textiles from different regions, bamboo basketry, soapstone carvings of animals and people and wood carvings.

THE BASICS

www.vimanmek.com
🔲 D4
✉ 16 Thanon Ratchawithi, Dusit
☎ 0 2228 6300
🕐 Tue–Sun 9.30–4.30 (ticket booth 9–3.15). Closed public holidays
🍴 Cafeteria in grounds and Thai restaurant near crafts shop
🚇 Phaya Thai then taxi
🚢 Tha Thewet pier
♿ Few
🎫 Free with entrance ticket for Grand Palace and Wat Phra Kaeo (▷ 24, 36)

HIGHLIGHTS

● Stained-glass panels
● Great architecture of the pavilion
● Tranquil garden

Baan Jim Thompson

HIGHLIGHTS

● Teak Ayutthaya architecture
● Exotic landscaped garden
● Views over the *khlong*
● Asian art collection
● Traditional Thai paintings

TIPS

● Photography is not allowed inside the house.
● Be aware that people linger outside and occasionally dupe visitors by claiming the house is shut and offering a shopping tour instead.

Although it is a great introduction to traditional Thai architecture, this house clearly shows Western influences. The landscaped garden offers a welcome surprise after bustling Siam Square.

The lost adventurer American architect Jim Thompson first came to Thailand during World War II. As he couldn't get used to his uneventful life back in New York after the war, he decided to make Thailand his home. Thai culture and crafts fascinated him, but the day he discovered some silk-weavers near his house (▷ 87, panel) his fortune was secured. He was already something of a legend when, in 1967, he disappeared during an afternoon walk in the Cameron Highlands in Malaysia, never to be seen again. Thompson's friend, the author

Clockwise from far left: The stairway and checkered tiled hall; Chinese doors leading to a bedroom; the house is set in lush gardens; interior views

William Warren, wrote a great account of his life and death, *Jim Thompson: The Legendary American of Thailand,* published in 1970.

Thai-style residence Thompson bought six traditional teak houses in northern and central Thailand, and had them reassembled in Bangkok as his residence, adding Western elements such as stairways and marble floors. The exterior walls were turned inside out to face the interior, and the garden was lovingly landscaped, creating the effect of an oasis.

A wonderful collection The house, kept as Thompson left it, makes an ideal setting for his small display of Asian art. The collection of traditional Thai paintings is one of the world's best and there are some rare Buddha images.

THE BASICS

www.jimthompsonhouse. com

🔁 E5

✉ 6 Soi Kasem San 2, off Thanon Rama I, Siam Square

☎ 0 2216 7368

🕐 Daily 9–5 (last guided tour at 5pm)

🍴 Small café

🚆 Skytrain National Stadium

🚫 None

🎟 Moderate (guided tours only)

Baan Kam Thieng

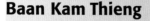

TOP 25

Kam Thieng House is set among formal gardens and trees

THE BASICS

www.siam-society.org

➕ G6

✉ 131 Soi Sukhumvit 21 (Soi Asoke)

☎ 0 2661 6470

🕐 Tue–Sat 9–5

🍴 Drinks in cafeteria

🚇 Skytrain Asoke

🚌 Sukhumvit

🖐 Moderate

♿ None

❓ The Siam Society has a library, gallery and small office selling its books. For lectures, check the website

HIGHLIGHTS

● Siam Society Library
● Floral lintels above the door to the inner room to ward off evil spirits

Kam Thieng House is a 19th-century teak stilthouse from Chiang Mai. Its collection focuses on the rural lifestyle of northern Thailand.

Lanna Living Museum Unlike Jim Thompson's House (▷ 74) and the Suan Pakkad Palace (▷ 81), Baan Kam Thieng shows how ordinary people lived. It represents a complete northern Thai house with living quarters, kitchen, well, granary, rice pounder, spirit house and household objects and utensils used in everyday life. Farming tools and fish traps are displayed at street level, while upstairs rooms capture the rural lifestyle of 160 years ago. The house was built by the granddaughter of a northern prince, and it is believed that her spirit and those of her mother and granddaughter still inhabit the house: There are many stories of inexplicable incidents occurring here.

Saengaroon House Saengaroon House, originally from Ayutthaya, contains the craft collection of the Thai architect Saengaroon Ratagasikorn, who studied in the US under Frank Lloyd Wright.

Siam Society The lovely garden belongs to the Siam Society, which also has an excellent library, recommended for anyone interested in Thai culture (call before visiting). The society also supports a gallery, holds lectures and publishes books on Thai culture and nature as well as the *Journal of the Siam Society*.

The beautiful exterior of the royal mansion (below, middle); the grand entrance (right)

TOP 25

Phra Thi Nang Vimanmek

A tour through Vimanmek Palace, the world's largest golden teak mansion, and the landscaped gardens, gives an insight into the interests of the Thai royal family.

"The Palace in the Clouds" The three-story mansion was originally built in 1868 as a summer house on the island of Ko Si Chang. It was moved wholesale to Dusit in 1901 and reassembled. It soon became King Rama V's favorite palace and was used as the royal residence between 1902 and 1906. It was closed down in 1935 and remained in this state until Queen Sirikit organized its renovation and opened it in 1982 as a museum to mark Bangkok's bicentennial celebrations.

First bathroom Although European influence is clearly visible in the style, Vimanmek is built according to Thai traditions, using golden teak wood and not a single nail. Teak wood contains a special oil that makes it resistant to heat and heavy rains, and which also acts as an insect repellent. Among the possessions of Rama V on display are Thailand's first indoor bathroom and the oldest typewriter with Thai characters, as well as Thai ceramics, china and portraits.

Carriages and crafts The Royal Carriage Museum contains several carriages, mostly imported from Europe, which were popular at the time of King Rama V. The small Suan Farang Kunsai Mansion has oil paintings and photographs of Rama V and his family.

THE BASICS

www.vimanmek.com

✚ D4

✉ 193/2 Thanon Ratchawithi

☎ 0 2228 6300

🕐 Tue–Sun 9.30–4.30 (ticket booth 9–3.15). Closed public holidays

🍴 Cafeteria on grounds and Thai restaurant near crafts shop

🚢 Tha Thewet pier

💰 Moderate; free with entrance ticket for Grand Palace and Wat Phra Kaeo (▷ 24, 36)

HIGHLIGHTS

● Garden and pond
● Ivory objects in the library

TIPS

● Visitors wearing shorts, miniskirts, flip-flops or sleeveless shirts may not be admitted.
● Free hour-long guided tours are compulsory (in English, every half hour).

DUSIT, SIAM SQUARE AND SUKHUMVIT TOP 25

77

Saan Phra Phrom (Erawan Shrine)

TOP 25

Surrounded by the trendiest stores, the Erawan Shrine is something of a surprise. Yet the old and traditional ways of praying and making offerings blend in with the new and modern city culture. Classical Thai dancing is performed here for donations.

Spirit house The Erawan Shrine was erected as a spirit house connected to the Erawan Hotel, which has now made way for the Grand Hyatt Erawan Hotel. The forces of the typical Thai spirit house didn't seem effective enough during the building of the hotel, so spirit doctors advised that it be replaced with the four-headed image of Brahma (Phra Phrom in Thai). There have been no further hitches since then, and the shrine has became famous

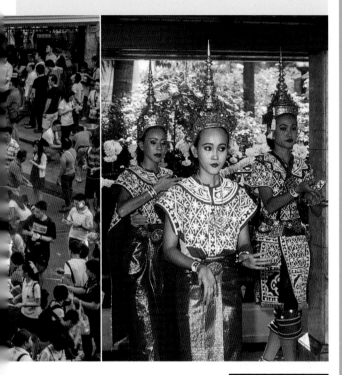

Worshipers laying offerings at the shrine (left); classical Thai dancers wearing traditional costume perform at Saan Phra Phrom (right)

for bringing good fortune. The name Erawan comes from Brahma's three-headed elephant.

Merit-making People come here to offer colorful flower garlands, lotus flowers, incense and candles; after a few minutes at the shrine your senses tend to go into overdrive. Often, if a wish has been granted, people thank the spirits by donating teak elephants or commissioning the classical dancers and live orchestra to perform. Outside the shrine women sell birds in tiny cages, which are believed to bring good fortune and earn merit if you set them free. The variety of worshipers here is also surprising: older people, Thai families with children, and fashionable younger women in the latest Western designer clothes all kneel down to perform the same traditional rites.

THE BASICS

➕ F6
✉ Corner of Thanon Ratchadamri and Thanon Ploenchit
🕐 Early morning to late night
🍴 Restaurants nearby
🚇 Skytrain Chit Lom or Ratchadamri
♿ Good
🎟 Free

Thanon Sukhumvit

Rush-hour traffic clogs Sukhumvit Road on a daily basis

THE BASICS

⊞ G6–K9
🍴 Numerous good restaurants
🚆 Skytrain Ploenchit, Nana, Asoke, Phrom Phong, Thong Lor, Ekkamai, Phra Kanong
♿ Few

DID YOU KNOW?

● *Thanon* means "road" or "street," *soi* means "small street" and *drok* means "little alley."
● Some *soi* are also known under their proper names—so, Sukhumvit Soi 21 is Soi Asoke.

Sukhumvit Road runs like a major artery through the heart of Bangkok. The area is a buzzy, lively and fun part of the city to explore.

Getting around The area has welcomed the arrival of some extremely high-end luxury and boutique hotels. The many *soi* that branch off Sukhumvit are home to hotels, restaurants and bars, tailors and trendy nightclubs, as well as catering to those in the search of Bangkok's more infamous forms of entertainment.

Shopping galore The seemingly endless street of Sukhumvit, and the *soi* off it, have all the shopping in the world. (The area is served by the safe and cheap Skytrain so you can avoid the traffic.) Around Soi 11 are several crafts shops with good tourist items. Soi 23 has some better crafts shops with Thai produce. The huge Emporium Shopping Complex combines Western and Thai designer stores (▷ 86), while H.M. Factory for Thai Silk (▷ 87) on Soi 39 is good for ties, scarves and accessories. Thong Lor or Soi 55 remains noted for its cool bars and restaurants.

Entertainment Much of the city's nightlife now happens in the *soi* off Sukhumvit Road. Some of the most on-trend bar-clubs are on Soi 8, 11 and Soi Siam Square 6, including Bed Supperclub (▷ 90) and Det-5 (▷ 90). For a different atmosphere head for Little Arabia around Soi 3 and Soi 5.

Wang Suan Pakkad

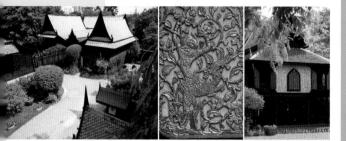

Suan Pakkad Palace is a lovely corner amid urban sprawl. Like Jim Thompson (▷ 74), its owners were passionate and discerning collectors of Thai arts and traditional architecture.

"Cabbage Farm Palace" Prince and Princess Chumbhot of Nakhon Sawan moved these eight traditional Thai houses from Chiang Mai (some had belonged to the prince's great-grandfather) in 1952. The cabbage garden was turned into one of Bangkok's finest landscaped gardens and is calm in a uniquely Eastern way. The princess was one of the country's most dedicated art collectors, and the house has been turned into a museum displaying every-day objects such as perfume bottles and musical instruments. Antiques include an exquisite Buddha head from Ayutthaya, Khmer statues and European prints of old Siam.

Ban Chiang House An entire house is devoted to the elegant pottery and bronze jewelry discovered at Ban Chiang, an important Bronze Age settlement in northern Thailand, dating from around 1600–500BC.

Lacquer Pavilion The exquisite Lacquer Pavilion, once part of an Ayutthaya monastery, was moved here in 1959. The remarkable gold and black lacquer murals depict events from the life of the Buddha and the *Ramakien*, the Thai version of the *Ramayana* epic. The lower layer is notable for its representations of daily life.

THE BASICS

www.suanpakkad.com
+ F5
✉ Thanon Sri Ayutthaya
☎ 0 2245 4934
⏰ Daily 9–4
🍴 Restaurants around Victory Monument
🚃 Skytrain Phaya Thai
♿ None
💰 Moderate

HIGHLIGHTS

● Lacquer Pavilion
● Buddha head from Ayutthaya
● Lovely enclosed garden
● Wonderful prints of old Siam by European artists

More to See

BAIYOKE TOWER II

www.baiyokeskyhotel.com
Currently the second Baiyoke Tower is the city's tallest building, and one of the world's highest hotels. The hotel occupies the 22nd to 50th floors, and there are observation decks on the 77th and 84th floors. Go on a clear day for sweeping views over the city. The glass elevator shoots up a corner of the building, and is definitely not recommended for those scared of heights.
🔼 F5 ✉ Thanon Ratchaprarop, Prathunam ☎ 0 2656 3000 🕐 Daily 10.30–10.30 🍴 Moderate 🚇 Skytrain Phaya Thai

BANGKOK DOLL FACTORY

www.bangkokdolls.com
Come here to see Khunying Tongkorn Chandevimol's private collection of dolls from her own factory and all over the world. Family members make the fine Thai dolls, inspired by Thai history and mythology, which are now sold all over the country.
🔼 F5 ✉ Soi Ratchataphan (Soi Mo Leng), off Thanon Ratchaprarop ☎ 0 2235 3008 🕐 Tue–Sat 8.30–5 🚇 Skytrain Victory Monument, then taxi 🍴 Free

BENJAKITI PARK

This much-needed 52-acre (21ha) green zone opened in celebration of Queen Sirikit's Sixth Cycle (72nd birthday). Work continues to expand the park with the planting of indigenous flora.
🔼 G7 ✉ Thanon Ratchadaphisek 🕐 Daily 5am–8pm 🚇 Sirikit Center

CHURCH OF THE IMMACULATE CONCEPTION

In 1567, Portuguese traders brought Christianity to the old capital of Ayutthaya, and soon after the first Christian missionaries also arrived. The French Catholic missionaries, who arrived much later in 1662, had a greater influence on the Catholic Church in Bangkok itself, but it was the Portuguese who founded one of the city's earliest churches, the Immaculate

Downtown, with Baiyoke Tower II and World Trade Centre in the background

Church of the Immaculate Conception

Conception Church in Samsen. The original church was built in 1674 during the reign of King Narai, but the present church dates from 1847. On the compound there is a smaller, older church known as Wat Noi, now used as a museum for religious relics.

➕ C3 ✉ 167 Soi Mitrakam Samsen, off Soi 11 Thanon Samsen, Dusit ☎ 0 2243 2617, ext.167 🕐 Daily 8am–4pm, church 6–8pm 👣 Free 🚢 Tha Thewet pier

MUSEUM OF FLORAL CULTURE

www.floralmuseum.com

Housed within a century-old home and gardens, this museum from the highly regarded Thai floral designer Sakul Intakul looks at the importance attached to flowers and their use in religious and royal ceremonial occasions, as well as in everyday Thai life.

➕ D3 ✉ Samsen Soi 28 off Nakorn Chasi ☎ 0 2669 3633 🕐 Tue–Sun 10–6 👣 Inexpensive 🚇 Skytrain Saphan Taksin then take the Orange Flag Chao Phraya Express Boat to Payap pier

NAI LERT PARK SHRINE

In the back garden of the stylish Nai Lert Hotel, next to the *khlong*, is a rather unusual lingam shrine. Several phalluses carved in stone or wood surround the spirit house built by millionaire businessman Nae Loet in honor of the female deity, who is thought to inhabit the old sacred banyan tree on that spot. The shrine is incredibly popular with young women as it is believed to help fertility.

➕ F5 ✉ Swissotel, Nai Lert Park Hotel, 2 Thanon Witthayu 👣 Free 🚇 Skytrain Ploenchit

ROYAL ELEPHANT MUSEUM

Alongside Vimanmek Palace (▷ 77), the two stables that once provided a home for the royal white elephants now make up a museum devoted to the role of elephants in Thailand's history and society. There are displays of equipment and information on the contribution elephants have made to society. The importance of white elephants is

Religious offerings at the garden courtyard of the Museum of Floral Culture

The Royal Elephant Museum

explained: The animals are albinos (more brown than white) whose rarity made them sacred and the property of the king. When a white elephant was spotted, and its authenticity accredited by experts, an elaborate ceremony accompanied its presentation to the king. Photographs of the proceedings are on show in the museum.

🔁 D4 ⊠ Thanon Ratchawithi ☎ 0 2228 6300 ⏰ Daily 9.30–3.15 🍴 Restaurants at Dusit Zoo 🚇 Phaya Thai then taxi 🚢 Tha Thewet pier ✋ Price included in entry to Vimanmek Palace (▷ 77)

SIAM OCEAN WORLD
www.siamoceanworld.com
Take an enthralling journey through the habitats of the southern oceans at this attraction, and encounter the weird and wonderful flora and fish that live in the sea. The sharks can be seen being fed twice a day.

🔁 F6 ⊠ B1-B2 Floor, Siam Paragon, 991 Thanon Rama I, Pathumwan
☎ 0 2687 2000 ⏰ Daily 10–9
✋ Expensive 🚇 Skytrain Siam

SIAM PARK CITY
www.siamparkcity.com
It's a little out of the city but this amusement, theme and water park will thrill children. It's popular with locals too so best visited on weekdays. Tickets can be booked online. Height restrictions apply for certain rides.

🔁 Off map ⊠ 203 Suan Siam Road, Kannayao ☎ 0 2919 7200 ⏰ Daily: Water Park 10–5; Theme Park 11–6 ✋ Moderate
ℹ️ Best reached by taxi from your hotel

WAT BENCHAMABOPHIT
The "Marble Temple" is built from Carrara marble in a blend of traditional Thai temple architecture and European designs. There is a collection of 53 Buddha images in the courtyard. It is a perfect place to watch religious festivals and moonlit processions. The monks don't go out seeking alms but are visited by merit-makers between 6 and 7am.

🔁 D4 ⊠ Corner of Thanon Si Ayutthaya and Thanon Rama V ☎ 0 2282 7413 ⏰ Daily 8–5.30 🍴 Foodstalls ✋ Inexpensive

A fretwork bridge spanning a pond at Wat Benchamabophit

Prathunum

Discover an interesting mix of buildings, old and new, where the slick urban lifestyle is never far from traditional rural ways.

DISTANCE: 2–2.5 miles (3.5–4km) **ALLOW:** 1.5 hours

START

NATIONAL STADIUM
✚ E6 🚇 Skytrain National Stadium

1 Follow Thanon Rama I to the west and note the National Stadium on your left, Thailand's main football stadium, with an art deco facade.

2 Cross Thanon Rama I and turn right into the narrow lane of Soi Kasem San II, with Jim Thompson's House (▷ 74) at the end. Retrace your steps down Soi Kasem and turn left on Thanon Rama I.

3 The Mahboonkrong Center, popular with teenagers and with a good food hall (▷ 87), is on the right. Cross Thanon Phaya Thai, and ahead lies the lively Siam Square.

4 Return to Thanon Phaya Thai, and turn left. Walk to Chulalongkorn University, with an interesting mix of buildings set in a beautiful garden with a lake and an art gallery.

END

SUAN PAKKAD PALACE
✚ F5 🚇 Skytrain Phaya Thai

8 Back on Thanon Ratchaprarop, walk left on Thanon Sri Ayutthaya past Suan Pakkad Palace (▷ 81). Head to Phaya Thai Skytrain station.

7 Walk up Thanon Ratchadamri, across Thanon Phetburi, and find to the left Prathunum market on Thanon Ratchaprarop, with food stands, tailors and clothing shops. Back on Thanon Ratchaprarop, walk left and take the first street to the left to find the Baiyoke Tower II (▷ 82).

6 Turn right on Rama I again and find, on the junction, the Erawan shrine (▷ 78).

5 Walk out on Henri Dunant Road, turn left and go to the end of the road.

DUSIT, SIAM SQUARE AND SUKHUMVIT WALK

Shopping

ALMETA

www.almeta.com

Almeta specializes in weaving to order and monogramming bed linens. You can buy Thai silks in hundreds of shades and weights here, as well as sumptuous silk wallpaper.

✚ H6 ✉ 20/3 Soi 23 Thanon Sukhumvit ☎ 0 2204 1413 🚇 Skytrain Asoke
Ⓜ Sukhumvit

L'ARCADIA

L'Arcadia is a small store with well-priced antique furniture and carved teak architectural ornaments, mainly from Thailand and Myanmar (Burma).

✚ H6 ✉ 12/2 Soi Sukhumvit 23 ☎ 0 2259 9595 🚇 Skytrain Asoke
Ⓜ Sukhumvit

CELADON HOUSE

This is the place to see the largest selection of celadon ware, from the Chiang Mai factory, in all shapes and colors. Check out the bargains in the back room.

✚ G–H7 ✉ 8/6–8 Soi Ratchadaphisek (Soi 16), Sukhumvit ☎ 0 2229 4383 🚇 Skytrain Asoke
Ⓜ Sukhumvit

EMPORIUM SHOPPING COMPLEX

www.emporiumthailand.com

This huge shopping center is definitely the place to come for all the designer brands of the moment, including Prada, MiuMiu, Shanghai Tang

and Louis Vuitton, plus less expensive labels such as Jaspal and Stefanel. There is an amazing food hall on the fifth floor and a large fresh fruit and vegetables area where you can buy exotic Thai fruits and fresh herbs. Counters sell ready-made Thai desserts and delectable snacks.

✚ H7 ✉ Soi Sukhumvit 24 🚇 Skytrain Phrom Phong

EXOTHIQUE THAI

A huge selection of Thai crafts is available at Exothique, which has a contemporary vibe. This is a great place to stock up on celadon plates, organic spa products with Thai herbs, relaxing Thai cushions as well as ethnic-inspired silk clothing.

✚ H7 ✉ 4th floor, Siam Paragon (panel, ▷ below) ☎ 0 2664 8000, ext. 1554 🚇 Skytrain Phrom Phong

SIAM PARAGON

The latest and glitziest of all shopping malls is the Siam Paragon, with all the major international designer labels, a huge department store, a floor dedicated to Thai crafts and design, and a vast cinema complex. www.siamparagon.co.th
✚ F6 ✉ 991 Thanon Rama I, Siam Square
☎ 0 2610 8000
🕐 Daily 10–10
🚇 Skytrain Siam Square

GAYSORN PLAZA

www.gaysorn.com

An exclusive shopping center that is all about glittering marble floors, top designer labels and an incredibly well-heeled clientele.

✚ F6 ✉ Corner of Thanon Ploenchit and Thanon Ratchadormi 🚇 Skytrain Chit Lom

GEO

www.geo.co.th

Buy home decor products and gifts designed and produced exclusively in Thailand at this stylish shop. The range includes ceramics, jewelry, bags, stationery and scarves.

✚ J6 ✉ 912/3 Sukhumvit 55 ☎ 0 2331 4324
🚇 Skytrain Thong Lo

GOOD SHEPHERD

www.goodshepherdbangkok.com

The Good Shepherd's Fatima Shop has a wide range of handicrafts and embroidery for sale from producer groups and crafts people across Thailand. The money received goes to support the Good Shepherd Sisters ministries and helps to improve the lives of people and families whose work is sold.

✚ H7 ✉ 591/17 Sukhumvit Soi 22 ☎ 0 2245 0457
🚇 Skytrain Phrom Phong

GREYHOUND

www.greyhound.co.th

Greyhound sells chic and contemporary casual wear

for men and women plus a more edgy collection, called Playhound by Greyhound, for younger people.

 F6 ✉ Siam Center, and branches on Rama I ☎ 0 2251 4917 🚇 Skytrain Siam

HERRMANN FASHIONS

www.herrmannsuits.com
Herrmann Fashions has been trading on the same premises for almost a quarter of a century. Custom-made tailoring is the stock in trade but it's also a good place if you want to buy Thai silk.

🗺 G6 ✉ 73/1 Sukhumvit, Soi 3 ☎ 0 2252 3917 🚇 Skytrain Nana

H.M. FACTORY FOR THAI SILK

www.hmfactory-thaisilk.com
Mr Pipat Vanijvongse built a small silk factory and a showroom in his house in 1957 and it's still going strong. As well as purchasing scarves, ties, cushions and accessories made from the finest Thai silk customers can also see the manufacturing process at work.

🗺 J8 ✉ 45 Soi Promchai, Sukhumvit Soi 39 ☎ 0 2258 8766 🚇 Skytrain Phrom Phong

JIM THOMPSON FACTORY OUTLET STORE

If you're looking for products from the Jim Thompson range then make for its factory outlet

store. The company also has outlets in Phuket, Pattaya and Nakhon Ratchasima.

🗺 Off map ✉ 153 Sukhumvit 93 ☎ 0 3326 5304 🚇 Skytrain Bang Chak

KINOKUNIYA

Bangkok's largest and best English bookstore sells a wide range of both locally printed and imported books.

🗺 H7 ✉ 3rd floor, Emporium Shopping Complex, 622 Thanon Sukhumvit, Soi 24 ☎ 0 2664 8554 🚇 Skytrain Phrom Phong

LA LANTA FINE ARTS

www.lalanta.com
This respected gallery focuses on contemporary Asian art as well as internationally recognized talent. It also runs a youth program designed to seek out, nurture and promote the work of exciting young artists from countries across Asia.

🗺 H7 ✉ 245/14 Sukhumvit Soi 31 ☎ 0 2260 5381 🚇 Skytrain Phrom Phong

MAHBOONKRONG (MBK) CENTER

www.mbk-center.co.th
You can buy everything from knockoff designer labels to mobile phone accessories at this shopping mall (particularly lively on weekends). Stores range from teenage favorites to the more upscale Tokyu department store. There is a good food court here too.

🗺 E6 ✉ Corner of Thanon Rama I and Thanon Phaya Thai 🚇 Skytrain National Stadium or Siam Square

NARAI PHAND

www.naraiphand.com
Huge crafts and souvenir emporium. Usually good value.

🗺 F6 ✉ 127 Thanon Ratchadamri, north of Thanon Gesorn ☎ 0 2252 4670 🚇 Skytrain Chit Lom

NARRY TAILOR

www.narry.com
Voted Bangkok's "Tailor of the Year" for several years running. Good-quality

work and quick service. Phone for a free pick-up.

➕ G6 ✉ 155/22 Thanon Sukhumvit Soi 11/1, near Swiss Park Hotel ☎ Mobile 0 818347545 🚈 Skytrain Nana

PANTHIP PLAZA

A huge shopping mall with seven floors dedicated to computer hardware, software, pirated versions of everything and all the latest gadgets.

➕ F5 ✉ 604/3 Thanon Rachathewi 🚈 Skytrain Chit Lom, then take a taxi or walk

PAPAYA

This vast warehouse is filled with some of the most stylish furniture from the past 100 years. It's is hard to find but well worth the trouble. Walk up Thanon Ratchadamri and leave Gaysorn Plaza to your right. Go under the second pedestrian walkway and turn right at the Citizen Building. Continue until you find Seefah Restaurant; Papaya is on the opposite side of the road, up the steep ramp.

➕ F5 ✉ 89/57 Bangkok Bazaar, Thanon Ratchadamri ☎ 0 2655 3355 🚈 Skytrain Chit Lom

PIRUN THONG

Looking for some different furnishings to take home and add a touch of Thai style to your home? This shop offers a range of pillows, curtains, throws and lamp shades

ready made or produced to order.

➕ J8 ✉ Sukhumvit Soi 45–47 ☎ 0 2258 7296 🚈 Skytrain Phrom Phong

PRAYER TEXTILE GALLERY

www.prayertextilegallery.com
You can buy old and new traditional textiles from northern Thailand, Laos and Cambodia at this gallery, as well as some ready-made garments.

➕ J8 ✉ Sukhumvit Soi 45–47 ☎ 0 2258 7296 🚈 Skytrain Phrom Phong

PROPAGANDA

www.propagandaonline.com
A bright and cheerful place in the Emporium Shopping Complex (▷ 86) that sells funky designs with a humorous twist. Look out for the shark bottle opener, the plastic homeware and bright T-shirts.

➕ F5 ✉ 4th Floor, Emporium Shopping Complex ☎ 0 2658 0430 🚈 Skytrain Siam

SPIRIT HOUSES

Several open-air stores sell spirit houses—a small version of a traditional Thai house where the guardian spirit resides—and accessories in all sizes and colors.

➕ G5 ✉ Thanon Phetburi, just past expressway bridge 🚌 A/C bus 502

RASI SAYAM

www.rasisayam.com
This old wooden house is filled with wonderful Thai handicrafts, pottery, baskets, woodwork and textiles—some old, some very contemporary—but all ranges are carefully selected and all are reasonably priced.

➕ H6 ✉ 82 Sukhumvit Soi 33 ☎ 0 2262 0729 🚈 Skytrain Phrom Phong 🚇 Sukhumvit

ROBINSON

www.robinson.co.th
Robinson's is an institution in Bangkok with several branches around the city, including Sukhumvit. Whatever you need, whether it be undies, toiletries, gifts or clothes, you can find it here at bargain prices.

➕ G6 ✉ 259 Sukhumvit, North Klongtoey, Wattana ☎ 0 2252 5121 🚈 Skytrain Asoke or Nana

TAILOR ON TEN

www.tailoronten.com
It may not be the cheapest tailor in a part of town where there's (at least) one on each corner, but Tailor on Ten has established an international reputation for its in-house tailoring, fine fabrics and designs that reflect both traditional and modern styling. Despite its name, it is actually on Sukhumvit Soi 8.

➕ G9 ✉ 93 Sukhumvit Soi 8 ☎ 0848 771 543 🚈 Skytrain Nana

Entertainment and Nightlife

BACCHUS

www.bacchus-winebar.com
Bacchus is one of the trendiest places to be seen in Bangkok. It's a multi-level wine bar offering a range of wines and spirits and regular tasting events. The relaxing top floor has a glass ceiling where you can enjoy the night sky.
🚹 G6 ✉ 20/6-7 Ruam Rudee, Ploenchit, Pathumwan ☎ 0 2650 8986 🕓 4pm–1am 🚉 Skytrain Ploenchit

BANGKOK OPERA

www.bangkokopera.com
This company—which presents the best of the international opera repertoire and some home-grown favorites—performs at locations across town, primarily the Thailand Cultural Centre. Visit the website to view the latest schedule and obtain tickets.

BED SUPPERCLUB

www.bedsupperclub.com
A hot spot in town, this is a white space capsule with an interior reminiscent of a Stanley Kubrick film. Recline on the beds while enjoying the consistently good Pacific Rim fusion food cooked by the talented American chef. Later the DJ spins laid-back dance music, but it's hard to find a space to dance. Minimum admission age 20. ID required.
🚹 G6 ✉ 26 Sukhumvit Soi 11 ☎ 0 2651 3537

🕓 7.30pm–2am
🎟 Admission charge
🚉 Skytrain Nana

BRITISH COUNCIL

www.britishcouncil.or.th
The most active of the foreign cultural centers in Bangkok. Regular lectures, movies, concerts, music and dance.
🚹 E–F6 ✉ 254 Chulalongkorn Soi 64, Siam Square, off Thanon Phaya Thai ☎ 0 2657 5678 🕓 Daily 9.30am–6pm 🚉 Skytrain Siam Square

CHEAP CHARLIE'S

Bizarre, surreal and certainly unique, this little bar attracts both tourists and locals and is pretty unprepossessing at first glance. However, the drinks are cheap, the atmosphere lively and the decor boasts oddities (from buffalo skulls

---

GAY BARS

Silom Soi 2 and Soi 4 are the center of Bangkok's gay scene (you may need to provide proof that you are over 18 at establishments here). Babylon Bangkok (34 Soi Nandha, South Sathorn Road, tel 0 2679 7984) is a gay sauna, over four floors, often mentioned as one of the top 10 gay saunas in the world. Freeman (on a tiny *soi* off Soi 2, Thanon Silom) is said to have the best drag show (*kathoey*) in town.

---

to beehives and tribal masks) collected over its 20-year history.
🚹 G6 ✉ Sukhumvit Soi 11 (take the first left) ☎ 0 2253 4648 🕓 Mon–Sat 5pm–12.30am 🚉 Skytrain Asok

DET-5

www.det-5.com
Noted for its relaxed atmosphere and live music scene, Det-5 is popular with both tourists and the city's expats. It serves food (Thai and international) throughout the day and has an open-mic night on Mondays (from 8.30pm), instruments provided.
🚹 G6 ✉ 41 Sukhumvit Soi 8 ☎ 0 2653 1232 🕓 Daily 10pm–2am 🎟 Admission charge 🚉 Skytrain Nana

GLOW

A packed diary has assured this boutique bar and club a reputation for showcasing the best electronic music. The offering changes nightly and the experience is a mix of intimate style, dramatic lighting and funky decor.
🚹 G6 ✉ 96/4–5 Sukhumvit Soi 23 ☎ 0 2261 4446 🕓 Daily 7pm to late 🎟 Varies 🚉 Skytrain Asok

HANRAHANS

www.hanrahansbangkok.com
Bangkok certainly hasn't missed the global invasion of the Irish bar and if you're on the look out for familiar brews, excellent sports coverage, live music and a bit of the old

craic then Hanrahans is one of the best in town.
⊞ G6 ⊠ Sukhumvit Soi 4 ☎ 0 2255 0644 🚇 Skytrain Nana

THE LIVING ROOM
www.thelivingroombangkok.com
Offering fabulous jazz and an impressive cocktail list, The Living Room mixes comfort with style and is one of the city's most alluring hotel bars. It also offers a Grande Afternoon Tea (Saturday 3–8pm) and is said to have one of Bangkok's best Sunday brunches.
⊞ G6 ⊠ Sheraton Grande Sukhumvit, 250 Sukhumvit ☎ 0 2649 8353 🚇 Skytrain Asok

NATIONAL STADIUM
Venue for important *takraw* matches.
⊞ E6 ⊠ Thanon Rama I ☎ 0 2214 0121 🕔 Check locally for dates

THE OFFICE
www.theofficebkk.com
Aussie-run sports bar with live sports from the UK and Australia including Premier League football, rugby union, Australian football, cricket test matches and Formula 1.
⊞ H7 ⊠ Sukhumvit Soi 33 ☎ 0 2662 1936 🕔 Mon–Thu 3pm to late, Fri–Sun noon to late 🚇 Skytrain Phrom Phong

Q-BAR
www.qbarbangkok.com
Extremely popular bar-cum-club, with some of the best DJs in town. New York-style hip.
⊞ G6 ⊠ 34 Soi Sukhumvit 11 ☎ 0 2252 3274 🕔 8pm to late 🎟 Admission charge weekends only 🚇 Skytrain Nana

SIAM NIRAMIT
www.siamniramit.com
On offer here is a spectacular extravaganza with more than 150 performers taking the audience on a journey through Siamese history using state-of-the-art special effects to create a "fantasialike" production.
⊞ J4 ⊠ 19 Thanon Tiamruammit, Huaykwang ☎ 0 2649 9222 🕔 Daily shows at 8pm 🚇 Thailand Cultural Centre

SOI COWBOY
Elements of Bangkok's nightlife are infamous but for the most part it's

<table>
<tr><td>OFF TO THE MOVIES</td></tr>
</table>

Thai movies are often comedies, or karate or violent, all interlaced with intrigue and drama. Many movie theaters now show movies with English soundtracks or subtitles. To see original uncut versions, head for one of the cultural centers listed below. Bangkok boasts a number of luxury multiplex cinemas—the main chain in the city and across Thailand is Major Cineplex (www.majorcineplex.com).

all done with humor and you're unlikely to experience much in the way of hassle. Soi Cowboy, a short street with around 40 or so mostly—but not exclusively—go-go bars is a good choice if you want to satisfy your curiosity but avoid the more full-on clubs and bars of Nana Plaza and Patpong.
⊞ H6/7 ⊠ Sukhumvit between Soi Asoke (Sukhumvit Soi 21) and Sukhumvit Soi 23 🕔 Daily til late 🚇 Skytrain Asok

SPA 1930
www.spa1930.com
A full range of massage, spa and beauty treatments is available at this delightful spa. They'll even create one especially to deal with the mental and bodily fatigue of jetlag.
⊞ G6 ⊠ 42 Soi Tonson, Lumphini ☎ 0 2254 8606 🕔 Daily 9.30am–9.30pm; advance reservation recommended 🚇 Skytrain Pluenchit

THAILAND CULTURAL CENTRE
Come to this modern theater venue for concerts by the Bangkok Symphony Orchestra, as well as drama and classical Thai dance.
⊞ H4 ⊠ Thanon Ratchadaphisek, Huai Khwang ☎ 0 2247 0028 🕔 Telephone for performance dates 🚇 Thailand Cultural Centre (free shuttle bus to center on performance days)

Restaurants

PRICES	
Prices are approximate, based on a 3-course meal for one person.	
$$$	more than 2,000B
$$	1,000B–2,000B
$	under 1,000B

ANA'S GARDEN ($–$$)

Amid skyscrapers, this garden restaurant offers a welcome retreat from the city among lush palm trees. The food is traditional Thai.

➕ J7 ✉ 67 Soi 55 Sukhumvit ☎ 0 2391 1762 🕐 Daily 5am–midnight 🚊 Skytrain Thong Lor

BAN KHUN MAE ($–$$)

www.bankhunmae.com
Expect straightforward but well-prepared Thai food at Ban Khun Mae. The restaurant is popular with young Thais and families.

➕ E–F6 ✉ 458/6-9 Siam Square Soi 8, Rama I Road ☎ 0 2658 4112 🕐 11am–10pm 🚊 Skytrain Siam Square

BASIL ($$$)

www.basilbangkok.com
This trendy Thai restaurant serves excellent traditional and home-style cuisine in a contemporary setting. It looks like a beautiful deli with jars filled with curries and marinades, and a floor-to-ceiling rack filled with a selection of wine from all over the world. At the entrance is a large counter where the chef prepares Thai dishes. Keep some space for the mouthwatering desserts.

➕ G6 ✉ Sheraton Grande Sukhumvit, 250 Thanon Sukhumvit ☎ 0 2649 8366 🕐 Daily 12–2.30, 6–10.30, Sun Jazz brunch 12–3 🚊 Skytrain Asoke

BOURBON STREET ($$)

www.bourbonstbkk.com
New Orleans and Southern-style specials such as jambalaya, blackened red fish and pecan pie feature on the menu of this Cajun restaurant, and there is an American-style bar.

THE LOFT

This trendy food court, in a black minimalist interior with great lighting, has a plastic card paying system instead of the usual vouchers. Food stands sell Thai dishes, Vietnamese and Northern Thai as well as a few classy Western-style desserts, and everything tastes wonderful. It is 50 percent more expensive than the standard food court on the first floor, but definitely worth a visit.

➕ F6 ✉ Central Department Store, Thanon Ploenchit ☎ No phone 🕐 Daily 10–10 🚊 Skytrain Chit Lom 🚌 A/C bus 501, 508

➕ H7 ✉ 29/4–6 Washington Square, Soi Sukhumvit 22 ☎ 0 2259 0328 🕐 Daily 7am–1am 🚊 Skytrain Phrom Phong or Asoke

CRÊPES & CO. ($)

www.crepes.co.th
This is Bangkok's favorite crêperie in a beautiful Thai villa set in an exotic garden. The pancakes are delicious and hugely popular, but on offer also is a selection of salads and dishes covering the entire Mediterranean region. Great brunch.

➕ G7 ✉ 18/1 Sukhumvit Soi 12 ☎ 0 2653 3990 🕐 9am–midnight 🚊 Skytrain Asoke

DOSA KING ($)

www.dosaking.net
Dosa, thin crêpes made from lentil and rice batter, are the basis for the vegetarian meals served at this inexpensive eatery off Thanon Sukhumvit.

➕ G6 ✉ 153/7 Sukhumvit Soi 11 ☎ 0 2651 1651/2 🕐 Daily 11–11 🚊 Skytrain Nana

ENOTECA ITALIANA ($$)

Tucked away in a residential area, Enoteca Italiana could well be one of Bangkok's best kept culinary secrets. The food is said to be some of the best Italian in the city, the wine cellar is hugely impressive—and room must be reserved for the homemade ice creams.

✚ H7 ✉ 39 Sukhumvut Soi 27 ☎ 0 2258 4386 ⏰ Daily 6pm–midnight 🚆 Skytrain Phrom Phong 🚇 Sukhumvit

GOVINDA ($$)

Govinda is a good Italian vegetarian restaurant serving a wide range of salads, pastas and vegetable dishes.
✚ H7 ✉ 22 Mall Plaza, Sukhumvit Soi 22 ☎ 0 2663 4970 ⏰ Daily 6–11pm 🚆 Skytrain Phrom Phong

GREYHOUND CAFÉ ($$)

www.greyhoundcafe.co.th
Part of the Greyhound fashion house, this cool Western-style eatery offers a global menu including sashimi, salads and Thai dishes and is a great place for lunch.
✚ J7 ✉ J Avenue, Sukhumvit Soi 55 (or on 2nd floor of the Emporium Shopping Complex, (▷ 86) ☎ 0 2712 6547 ⏰ Daily 11am–10pm 🚆 Skytrain Thong Lor

INDUS ($$–$$$)

www.indusbangkok.com
Indian restaurants in Bangkok can be of variable quality but Indus, with its countless awards, modern interior (lovely garden dining area) and imaginative menu with a lighter, healthier twist, is a bit of a gem.
✚ H7 ✉ 71 Sukhumvit Soi 26 ☎ 0 2258 4900 ⏰ Daily 11.30–3, 6–11 🚆 Skytrain Phrom Phong

JE NGOR ($$)

The excellent cuisine at this Thai-Chinese seafood restaurant makes up for the somewhat unremarkable decor. Je Ngor, the Chinese owner, is so popular and famous for her dumplings that she has now opened several branches all over Bangkok.
✚ H7 ✉ 68/2 Sukhumvit Soi 20 ☎ 0 2258 8008 ⏰ Lunch, dinner 🚆 Skytrain Phrom Phong

KOI ($$$)

www.koirestaurantbkk.com
Koi LA and New York have come to Bangkok and how! Superb and

FOOD COURTS

Thais love eating their snacks or meals at food courts, usually located around shopping malls or office areas. The atmosphere is great sitting outside at night, while on a hot day the air-conditioned environment is a tempting option. Venues vary from the basic snack-type place found close to supermarkets to trendy upmarket food courts like the stylish Loft in Chit Lom. Food courts are a great way to sample a range of Thai dishes and flavors at small prices. Every stand or mini kitchen has its specialties, and ingredients are always fresh.

inventive Californian interpretations of Japanese delights are served in a dark, slick, minimalist interior. The bar and garden are filled with people nibbling on delicious little bites and sipping exotic cocktails.
✚ H7 ✉ 26 Sukhumvit Soi 20 ☎ 0 2258 1590 ⏰ Tue–Sun 6pm–midnight 🚆 Skytrain Asoke

KUPPA ($$)

www.kuppa.co.th
This trendsetting Australian-managed café, in a casual and spacious interior, is lively and buzzing at any time of the day. The food is a global mix of grills, salads and pastas, but do keep a space for the delicious homemade cakes.
✚ G–H7 ✉ 39 Sukhumvit Soi 16 ☎ 0 2259 1954 ⏰ Daily 10.30am–11.30pm 🚆 Skytrain Asoke

LAICRAM ($$)

This great restaurant offers superior and authentic Thai dishes, such as a delicious seafood curry, or Somtam (spicy green papaya salad), at surprisingly good prices. The interior is pretty straightforward, but both locals and tourists come here just to sample the excellent food.
✚ H6 ✉ Soi 23 Thanon Sukhumvit ☎ 0 2204 1069 ⏰ Daily 10–9 (until 3 on Sun) 🚆 Skytrain Asoke 🚇 Sukhumvit

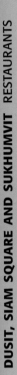

MAHANAGA ($$$)

www.mahanaga.com
Come here for inventive Thai-fusion cuisine complemented by a superb wine list. The interior decor is Moroccan inspired and there is a small courtyard-style garden. Great for a romantic night out, but book ahead.
🏠 H6 ✉ 2 Sukhumvit Soi 29 ☎ 0 2662 3060 🕐 Dinner 5.30–11pm, bar open til late 🚊 Skytrain Asoke

NIPPON TEI ($$$)

www.nippontei.com
Considered to be one of the best Japanese restaurants in town, Nippon Tei offers sashimi and sushi as well as Kobe beef and seafood.
🏠 F6 ✉ 161 Nantawan Bldg, Thanon Ratchadamri ☎ 0 2252 9438 🕐 Lunch, dinner 🚊 Skytrain Ratchadamri

RANG MAHAL ($$)

Some of the finest South Indian food in town is served here in pleasant and elegant surroundings, and accompanied by Indian classical music.
🏠 H7 ✉ Rooftop of Rembrandt Hotel, 19 Sukhumvit Soi 18 ☎ 0 2261 7100 🕐 Daily 6–11pm, Sun brunch buffet 11am–2.30pm 🚊 Skytrain Asoke

RUEN MALLIKA ($$)

A bit hard to find, but you are soon transported into another time when you do locate this converted teak house set in a lush garden. On the menu is excellent Thai cuisine, from the hot and spicy food from Southern Thailand to curries as served in the royal family. Recommended.
🏠 H7 ✉ Small soi off Soi 22 Thanon Sukhumvit ☎ 0 2663 3211 🕐 Daily 11–11 🚊 Skytrain Asoke

THE SPICE MARKET ($$–$$$)

www.fourseasons.com
The interior looks slightly dated but the food is still top notch at this friendly restaurant, from the soft shell crab curry or Pad Thai (Thai noodles) to the

MASSAMAN CURRY

Massaman curry is a staple on the menu of many restaurants in Thailand—but it is a dish with an interesting history. It is said to be an interpretation of a Persian dish, originating in Thailand in the 17th century at the court of Ayutthaya, although some claim it is from southern Thailand. The *massaman* curry also has regal connections, having been mentioned in a poem attributed to King Rama II (1767–1824). Typically made with chicken or beef, and accompanied by potatoes and roasted peanuts, it is served in a delicious aromatic broth.

home-style ice creams of coconut, tamarind or green tea.
🏠 F6 ✉ Four Seasons Bangkok, 155 Thanon Ratchadamri ☎ 0 2250 1000 🕐 Lunch, dinner 🚊 Skytrain Ratchadamri

VANILLA INDUSTRY RESTAURANT ($$)

www.vanillaindustry.com
This surprisingly retro-looking hot spot in a concept mall offers all-day dining, including all-day breakfast, delicious Western-style dishes as well as Thai bites. Afternoon tea is totally British with hot scones, muffins and pies.
🏠 J6 ✉ 818 Sukhumvit Soi 55 ☎ 0 2714 9652 🕐 Daily breakfast, lunch, dinner 🚊 Skytrain Thong Lor

VIENTIANE KITCHEN ($$)

www.vientiane-kitchen.com
This restaurant serves some of the most exciting food in town, mainly from Isaan province and Laos. The flavors are complex, intriguing and extremely delicious; really spicy if you want it to be. The service is peaceful and friendly, making the dining experience utterly pleasing. A live band plays traditional music, and with the open-air atmosphere really makes for a special evening.
🏠 J7 ✉ 8 Naphasap Yak 1, Sukhumvit Soi 36 ☎ 0 2258 6171 🕐 Daily noon–midnight 🚊 Skytrain Thong Lo

If the pace in the city gets to you, head out to the not-exactly-quiet Chatuchak Market, find rural Thailand in Bangkok's *khlongs*, or understand more of the country's history at Ayutthaya or at the River Kwai.

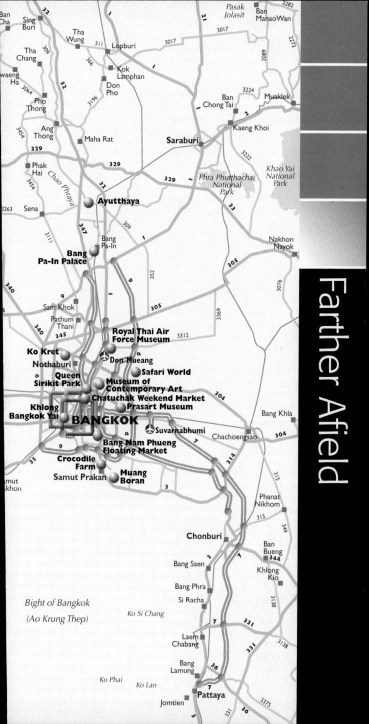

Chatuchak Weekend Market

HIGHLIGHTS

● Amulets and collectors' items, Section 1
● Antiques, Section 26
● Hill-tribe textiles and crafts, Section 24
● Aw Taw Kaw Market, royal project for organically grown produce on the other side of Thanon Phahonyothin

TIP

● Fatigue can kick in early, but there are several places to rest up and have a snack.
● Smoking is prohibited in the market.

This weekend market feels like the mother of all markets. You'll find everything from children's clothes to *mutmee* silk pajamas and antiques.

General view It used to take an hour (or even longer) to get to the market from the center, but it is now much faster with the expressway and, especially, with the Skytrain. Before going, get hold of Nancy Chandler's *Map of Bangkok* (available from English-language bookstores), which has a detailed map of Chatuchak showing what is for sale and where. Stalls are aimed at tourists and locals, who come here looking for food, plants, furnishings and trendy clothes.

Everything for sale If your time is limited, start with Soi 1, 2, 3 and 4 in Section 1, which sell

Visitors to the market can make a day of it—there is so much to see and buy, and if you need refreshments you'll find cafés and food vendors

antiques, wood carvings, musical instruments, hill-tribe items and crafts. The selection of sarongs in cotton and *mutmee* silk is amazing, while clothes by Thai designers are very wearable. The sections around the clock tower have mainly food supplies. Increasingly shops also sell vintage gear or copies of cult classics.

Illegal trade Regardless of a Thai law protecting endangered species, some products are still on sale in Chatuchak, branded "the wildlife supermarket of the world" by the Worldwide Fund for Nature. Very few endangered animals are still openly for sale in the market and, if they are, their cages will have signs insisting on "No Photograph." However, the black market is still thriving and you should be wary of suspicious dealers.

THE BASICS

www.chatuchak.org

➕ G2

✉ Thanon Phahonyothin, near Chatuchak Park

🕐 Sat, Sun 6–6

🍴 Foodstands and cafés throughout the market

🚇 Skytrain Mo Chit

🚌 Kamphaeng Phet

♿ None

🎟 Free

Khlong Bangkok Yai

HIGHLIGHTS

● Life and boats along the *khlongs*
● Murals in Wat Welurachin
● Wat Inthararam's painted doors
● Amulets from Wat Pak Nam

TIP

● Arrange with the boatman at any of the main piers to get you a long-tail boat and to tell the driver exactly what you want, at the same price you would get elsewhere.

A great way to escape Bangkok's busy traffic is to take to the water—a ride on the riverbus or a trip on the canals. Khlong Bangkok Yai leads from the Chao Phraya to the treasures of Thonburi.

From the river For many Bangkok residents, canals (*khlongs*) remain an important means of getting around the city and for the visitor they provide eye-opening views. The easiest and cheapest way of getting along Khlong Bangkok Yai is on one of the regular long-tail boats from either Tien or Rajinee piers on the Chao Phraya. On the right (north) bank as you enter the canal lies Wat Sang Krachai, dating from the Ayutthaya period and restored by early Chakri kings. As you pass under the first of Thonburi's main bridges, look for Wat Welurachin on the

Bangkok's canals are important to the city: They are a way of getting around without having to negotiate the busy roads, and many people live along them

left bank, with its 19th-century murals. Beyond the next bridge is Wat Inthararam (left bank), containing the ashes of King Taksin, who moved the Siamese capital to Thonburi in 1768, where he was deposed and killed 14 years later. It has beautiful lacquer decorations inside and out.

Back to the river At the junction of Khlong Sanam Chai and Bangkok Noi sits Wat Pak Nam, a huge temple from the Ayutthaya period, noted for its meditation center. From here Khlong Bangkok Yai curves north to meet Khlong Bang Noi (left) and Khlong Mon (right), which leads back to the Chao Phraya River. Across this junction, Khlong Bangkok Yai is called Khlong Chak Phra and leads to Khlong Bangkok Noi, and then to the Royal Barges Museum (▷ 28) and the Chao Phraya River.

THE BASICS

🕂 A7–B7

🍽 Floating foodstalls along the *khlong*

🚤 Regular boats from Tha Chang, Tha Tien; Tha Rajinee and Memorial Bridge piers

Prasart Museum

The traditional teak buildings here are a wonderful introduction to Thai culture

TOP 25

THE BASICS

➕ See map ▷ 97
✉ 9 Soi 4A, Thanon Krungthepkritha, off Thanon Srinakarintora, 97 Bang Kapi
☎ 0 2379 3601/7
🕐 Thu–Sun 10–3
💷 Expensive (includes a guide and a drink)
❓ Take a taxi (20–30 min from Siam Square). Admission by appointment only, so call ahead

HIGHLIGHTS

● Landscaped garden
● Red Palace
● Lanna-style Buddhas
● Benjarong ceramics

TIP

● Benjarong ceramics can be bought in the River City Shopping Complex (▷ 63).

It has been property tycoon Khun Prasart Vongsakul's mission to buy Thai antiques and objets d'art that had been sold abroad, and to restore them to Thailand. His museum is now an education and research center.

A private museum This rarely visited but superb collection is housed in an array of traditional Thai buildings, painstakingly reconstructed small temples, teak houses and palaces from all over Asia. The aim was to convey a flavor of the different Asian styles, not to create an exact reproduction. The delightful landscaped garden is home to some stunning Sukhothai-style terra-cotta pieces, and also has rare Thai and imported plants. This private museum in the Bang Kapi suburb gives a clear introduction to Thai art, architecture and history.

Many pavilions The golden teak Red Palace is an exquisite reproduction of the Tamnak Daeng, built in the Rama III period, now in the National Museum (▷ 27). Stunning antiques from the Ayutthaya and early Rattanakosin periods are found here, including furniture, and ornate gold vessels. The wooden Lanna Pavilion has a beautiful collection of Lanna-period Buddha images and a European-style mansion has period household utensils, beautiful Benjarong ceramics and Western art objects. Other buildings include a teak-wood library set over a lotus pond, a Lopburi-style chapel, a water garden and a Khmer Guanyin Shrine.

More to See

KO KRET

This tiny island is a world away from Bangkok, with wooden houses among the palm trees. The local pottery, *kwan arman*, is baked, unglazed red clay carved with intricate patterns. Temples include the Mon-style Wat Paramaiyikawat, with a marble Buddha.

🗺 See map ▷ 97 ✉ North of central Bangkok, near Nonthaburi 🍴 Several riverside restaurants 🚤 Chao Phraya Express boat to Nonthaburi, river taxi to Ko Kret

MUSEUM OF CONTEMPORARY ART

www.mocabangkok.com

Spread over five floors of a striking building with lots of natural light, the collection here consists of an eclectic mix of contemporary paintings and sculpture. There are also temporary exhibitions.

🗺 See map ▷ 97 ✉ 499 Kamphaengpet 6 Road, Ladyao, Chatuchak ☎ 0 2953 1005 🕐 Tue–Fri 10–5, Sat–Sun 11–6 💰 Moderate 🚇 Skytrain Mo Chit then taxi 🚉 Chatuchak Park then taxi

QUEEN SIRIKIT PARK

This park near Chatuchak Weekend Market (▷ 98) was built to commemorate the 60th birthday of the Queen. A golf course was transformed into a botanical garden for the conservation of Thai plants. The garden for the blind has signs in Braille. A pool winds its way through the park and the fountains in it entertain visitors three times a day.

🗺 G1–2 ✉ 820 Thanon Phahonyothin 🕐 Daily 5am–6pm 💰 Free 🚇 Skytrain Mo Chit 🚉 Kamphaeng Phet

SAFARI WORLD

www.safariworld.com

Thailand's largest zoo includes giraffes, lions and rhinos seen on a drive through the park, plus a marine park and bird area. Visitors can see tigers and lions being fed and get up close to giraffes on a head-height viewing platform.

🗺 See map ▷ 97 ✉ 99 Thanon Panyaintra, Samwatawantok, 5 miles (9km) from city center ☎ 0 2518 1000 🕐 Daily 9–5 💰 Expensive 🚇 Skytrain Mo Chit

Wat Paramaiyikawat stupa on Ko Kret Island

Portrait of HM Queen Sirikit

Excursions

THE BASICS

➕ See map ▷ 97
Distance: 46 miles (85km)
Journey Time: 1.5–2 hours
🚆 Regular trains (journey time 1.5 hours) from Hua Lamphong
🚌 Three buses an hour from Northern Bus Terminal Mo Chit
ℹ️ TAT Office, 108/22 Moo 4, Tambon Phratoochai, Amphoe Phra Nakhon Si ☎ 0 3524 6076. Boat tours available

AYUTTHAYA

When Bangkok was a small village, Ayutthaya was Thailand's capital, a glittering city on an artificial island encircled by canals, with scores of palaces, temples and over a million inhabitants.

For more than 400 years it was the capital of Siam, until 1767 when it was sacked by the Burmese. The old island city has been designated a UNESCO World Heritage Site and to get an overview of the scattered remains start off at the Historical Study Center (Thanon Rotchana, tel 0 3524 5124). Don't miss the temples of Wat Mahathat, Wat Ratburana, Viharn Phra Mongkol Bopit and Chantharakasem National Museum.

THE BASICS

www.palaces.thai.net
(▷ Ayutthaya, above)
🕐 Daily 8.30–4.30 (last tickets 3.30pm)
🖐 Moderate ❓ Shop

BANG PA-IN PALACE

In the mid-19th century at Bang Pa-In, the Thai royal family built a retreat. The palace incorporates classical Thai, Chinese and European architecture. Combine this with a visit to Ayutthaya and rent a golf cart to tour the site.

THE BASICS

➕ See map ▷ 97
✉️ Phra Pradaeng, Samut Praken Province
🕐 Sat–Sun 7–3
🍴 Foodstands on boats
🚤 Boat from Sam Phawut pier to Wat Bang Nam Phueng Nok then motorbike taxi or walk. Alternatively, take a taxi all the way from Bangkok

BANG NAM PHUENG FLOATING MARKET

This weekend market in Phra Pradaeng is easily reached by crossing the Chao Phraya River to an area known as the "green lung of Bangkok."

Most of the stalls are actually by the water rather than on it and the narrow lanes are perfect for a bit of exercise, so consider renting a bike. As a working market, it is popular with Thais searching for local specialties grown in the vicinity. Browse the foodstalls and then sample the freshly cooked food at wooden tables by the water.

CROCODILE FARM

Thailand's "Crocodile King," Mr Utai Youngprapakorn, founded the world's largest center to help preserve crocodiles.

There are more than 100,000 crocodiles at the farm consisting of 28 species, some of them no longer in existence elsewhere. The farm is mainly an education and research center for the conservation of wildlife, but it attracts the crowds by putting on Crocodile Wrestling and elephant shows, plus a zoo and a Dinosaur Museum.

THE BASICS

www.worldcrocodile.com
✚ See map ▷ 97
✉ 555 Moo 7, Taiban, Amphoe Muan, Samutprakarn (6 miles/10km) from Bangkok)
☎ 0 2703 4891
🕓 Daily 8–6
✋ Expensive
🚉 Skytrain Bearing then taxi

MUANG BORAN

This is a large open-air museum where more than 100 small versions of the most important Thai temples, palaces and traditional houses are spread over a Thailand-shaped area.

This could be tacky, but is actually well done and makes for a pleasant day out. Heat permitting, the lush tropical gardens are great for cycling and, since this is Thailand, food stalls and restaurants offer plenty of opportunities for snacks and drink.

THE BASICS

www.ancientcity.com
✚ See map ▷ 97
Distance: 20 miles (33km)
Journey Time: 2 hours
✉ 269/1 Sukhumvit Road, Bangpho, Samut Prakan
☎ 0 2323 4094 🕓 Daily 9–7 ✋ Expensive. Cycle rental 50B 🚉 Skytrain Bearing then taxi

NAKHON PATHOM

This sleepy town is home to Thailand's tallest Buddhist monument, the 394ft (120m) Phra Pathom Chedi.

The original was built by sixth-century Buddhists of Dvaravati, but the current structure dates from 1860. In the *bot* is an Ayutthaya-style Buddha seated in a European pose. The temple is one of the six most sacred temples in the country.

THE BASICS

✚ See map ▷ 96
Distance: 35 miles/56km west of Bangkok
🚌 Daily service from Thonburi's Southern Bus terminal
🚆 Trains 8.05, 9.20am; more in the afternoon from Hua Lamphong station

THE BASICS

See map ▷ 96
Distance: 79 miles (130km) from Bangkok
Journey Time: 2–3 hours
Two trains daily for Kanchanaburi from Bangkok Noi Railway Station
Buses from Bangkok's Southern Bus Terminal, Thonburi (every 20 min until late evening)
TAT office, Thanon Sangshuto

RIVER KWAI

The focus of the movie *The Bridge on the River Kwai*, the Death Railway was built by Allied prisoners of war and Asian laborers in the 1940s with the loss of many thousands of lives, then rebuilt after the war.

A tourist train now runs along the tracks. Kanchanaburi, the town near the bridge, is the site of the JEATH War Museum and the Kanchanaburi War Cemetery, the last resting place of 6,982 Allied prisoners of war. The Chung Kai War Cemetery contains the graves of 1,750 of the estimated 16,000 Allied prisoners of war who died during construction of the railway.

THE BASICS

See map ▷ 97
171 Paholyothin Road, Don Muang Airport
Daily 8–4 Free
From Hua Lamphong to Don Muang station then taxi

ROYAL THAI AIR FORCE MUSEUM

Aviation started in Thailand with demonstration flights during 1911, and later that year, three Thai Army officers were sent to France to train as aviators.

This museum has a great collection of airplanes including a Cessna 0-1 Bird Dog, a Douglas Skyraider and a Vought V-935 Corsair, the last one remaining in the world.

THE BASICS

www.siamwinery.com
See map ▷ 97
Distance: 31 miles (50km)
9/2 Moo 3 Tumbon Bangtorud, Mueang District, Samut Sakhon
0 3484 5334
Mon–Sat tours at 10am and 2pm
Expensive From Southern Terminal, Bangkok

SIAM WINERY

Southeast Asia's largest vineyard was established in 1986 by Chalerm Yoovidhya.

This is close to floating vineyards where farmers grow the local Malaga Blanc and Red Pokdum grapes. The wines have now won several awards and are becoming recognized internationally. Tours include the vineyard, the wine-making process and wine tasting. The winery also cultivates grapes at two other vineyards in the country. One is located in the Huan Hin Hills and the other in the Pak Chong Hills.

Bangkok has a wide range of hotels from the most luxurious to the absolute basic, but as traffic is so often at a standstill it pays to book a hotel in the area of the city where you are likely to spend more time.

Where to Stay

Introduction

Accommodations are spread around the city in clearly defined areas and it pays to think about which area best suits your itinerary in the capital.

The Choices

If you want to spend a lot of time shopping and dining out and require good transportation connections, then Thanon Sukhumvit and the *soi* that run off it are worth considering. Budget-wise, this is a mid-range area but it also has some top-class hotels like the Four Seasons as well as good-value budget places like Suk 11. For the luxury hotel experience you need to stay by the river or, for chic places like the Met and the Sukhothai, along the top end of Thanon Sathorn Tai. Banglamphu and the Thanon Khao San area are good for budget accommodations, but there are also some good mid-range places here and the area is convenient for the Grand Palace, National Museum and Dusit.

What to Expect

Rates at all the hotels vary according to demand and time of year, falling during the rainy season and escalating in the high season, rising even higher if there is a big festival or event in town. Apart from at quality hotels, it is normal practice to be shown your room before you agree to stay. In budget places you should check the shower and hot water and door locks, and if appropriate the availability of mosquito nets and how well the windows close. Nonsmoking rooms are more common now, but do check.

VIEW OVER THE RIVER

The traditional place to stay, and the most peaceful, is by the river, either in the Mandarin Oriental or the equally excellent Peninsula right across the river. The River View Guest House is a good budget choice, but there are few other inexpensive options. The advantage of staying close to the river is that you can avoid traffic jams. Sights like the temples and the Grand Palace can be visited by boat, and you can take the hotel shuttle boat to the Skytrain station.

Stay in a traditional teak house or plush new hotel—you're sure of a warm welcome

Budget Hotels

PRICES

Expect to pay under 1,500B per night for a budget hotel.

ATLANTA

www.theatlantahotel.bangkok.com
Atlanta is a popular old-fashioned 1950s hotel on central Sukhumvit with simply decorated, air-conditioned or fan rooms and a swimming pool. The hotel has a reputation for friendly service and appeals to families.
➕ G6 ✉ 78 Soi Sukhumvit 2 ☎ 0 2252 6069
🚇 Skytrain Ploenchit

BANGKOK CHRISTIAN GUESTHOUSE

www.bcgh.org
This is a lovely Christian-based guesthouse with wonderful staff, 57 simple but very tidy rooms and a great, lush lawn with a fish pond.
➕ F7 ✉ 123 Soi Sala Daeng 2, off Thanon Convent, Silom ☎ 0 2233 6303 🚇 Skytrain Sala Daeng

BOONSIRI PLACE

www.boonsiriplace.com
Close to the Grand Palace and Wat Pho, the 48 rooms here boast contemporary Thai decor, each room decorated with different oil paintings depicting various cultural styles.
➕ C5 ✉ 55 Buranasart Road, Prankorn ☎ 0 2622 2189 ⛴ Tha Chang pier

CHARLIE HOUSE

www.charliehousethailand.com
The modest, but comfortable rooms here, just 18 in total, all have air-conditioning, satellite TV and free WiFi. A good value guesthouse in a great location.
➕ F7 ✉ 1034/36–37 Soi Saphan Khu ☎ 0 2679 8330 🚇 Lumphini

RIVER VIEW GUEST HOUSE

www.riverviewbkk.com
This place has spacious rooms overlooking the Chao Phraya. A good breakfast of cereal and fresh fruit is served on the top floor.
➕ D7 ✉ 768 Soi Phanurangsri, Songwad Road,

THANON KHAO SAN

First came backpackers in search of the pleasures of the Orient, then local Thais and Chinese who saw the possibilities. Thanon Khao San and its neighborhood is now the place for cheap beds, low-cost eats, low-cost clothes and low-cost beer. If you're on a tight budget, this is the place to be, but arrive early in the day if you want to find a bed. One thing's for sure, wherever you stay it's going to be lively. Thanon Khao San is now also popular with young Thais as the place to go for a beer in the evening.

Talad Noi ☎ 0 2234 5429 🚇 Hua Lamphong

SHANTI LODGE

www.shantilodge.com
A quiet hotel set in a garden, the Shanti Lodge has well-kept and air-conditioned rooms, all decorated in Thai style.
➕ C4 ✉ 37 Sri Ayudhya Road, Soi 16 (behind National Library) ☎ 0 2281 2497 ⛴ Tha Thewet

SUK 11

www.suk11.com
This is a family-run guesthouse in a wonderful wooden house, with clean air-conditioned rooms and dorms, and a lovely garden.
➕ G6 ✉ 1/13 Sukhumvit 11 ☎ 0 2253 5927 🚇 Skytrain Nana

VILLA GUEST HOUSE

Villa is another beautiful teak house in a lovely garden away from the noisy city streets. Shared bathrooms and lots of atmosphere.
➕ C4 ✉ 230 Soi, 1 Thanon Samsen ☎ 0 2221 7009 ⛴ Tha Phra Athit

WENDY HOUSE

www.wendyguesthouse.com
Friendly and near Siam Square, Wendy House offers clean, simple, spacious rooms with air-conditioning. Lower prices for longer stays.
➕ E–F6 ✉ 36/2 Soi Kasemsan 1, off Thanon Rama I ☎ 0 2214 1149 🚇 Skytrain National Stadium

Mid-Range Hotels

BEL-AIRE

www.belairebangkok.com
The Bel-Aire offers stylish, affordable luxury just a stone's throw from the hustle and bustle of Thanon Sukhumvit and a five-minute walk from the Skytrain. Bar, lounge, restaurant and pool.
🕂 G6 ✉ 16 Sukhumvit, Soi 5 ☎ 0 2253 4300
🚈 Skytrain Nana

BUDDY LODGE

www.buddylodge.com
The smartest hotel in the street, this boutique hotel offers comfortable rooms decorated with Thai designs and incorporating a lot of wood. The very laid-back atmosphere is in tune with the backpackers' haven outside.
🕂 C5 ✉ 265 Thanon Khao San ☎ 0 2629 4777
🚢 Tha Phra Athit pier

DREAM

www.dreambkk.com
An ultra-modern hotel where sleep is taken seriously in its 195 rooms as they are all lit by ethereal, sleep-inducing blue lights. The hotel also features a rooftop pool, restaurant and spa.
🕂 G6 ✉ Soi Sukhumvit 15 ☎ 0 2254 8500 🚈 Skytrain Nana

GRAND CHINA PRINCESS

www.grandchina.com
If you want to stay in Chinatown then this is the hotel to choose. The 155 rooms have all the necessary amenities and the hotel has a choice of places to eat, including a revolving restaurant at the top. There's also music in the lobby at night, a fitness center and a Thai massage service.
🕂 D6 ✉ 215 Thanon Yaowarat ☎ 0 2224 9977
🚇 Hua Lamphong 🚢 Tha Ratchawongse

HIP BANGKOK

www.hip-bangkok.com
Decorated in a funky, colorful contemporary style, this is a good-value choice if a central location isn't important, although it is close to a Metro station.
🕂 H3 ✉ 111/1 Soi Niam U-tit Ratchadaphisek Road, Dindaeng ☎ 0 2276 5777
🚇 Huay Kwang

IBRIK RESORT HOTEL ON THE RIVER

www.ibrikresort.com
This small three-room boutique hotel has a rare riverfront location with views of the Grand Palace. Very stylish rooms with air-conditioning, bathroom and balcony.
🕂 B5 ✉ 256 Soi Wat Rakang, off Thanon Arunamrin, Bangkok-noi ☎ 0 2848 9220
🚢 Cross-river ferry from Tha Chang to Tha Wat Rakang or Tha Wang Lang

JIM'S LODGE

www.jimslodge.com
A quiet, pleasant hotel located within easy walking distance of a choice of restaurants, Lumphini Park and shops, Jim's Lodge offers 75 rooms, all with air-conditioning, satellite TV and private bathrooms.
🕂 G6 ✉ 125/7 Soi Ruam Rudee, off Thanon Ploenchit Lumphini ☎ 0 2255 3100
🚈 Skytrain Ploenchit

LUXX

www.staywithluxx.com
One of two Luxx hotels in Bangkok—the other can be found in Langsuan—this small boutique hotel with just 13 rooms is close to the shopping, restaurant and nightlife scene of Silom. The design is contemporary and chic and the bathrooms have a signature wooden bathtub.
🕂 E7 ✉ 6/11 Decho Road, Bangruk ☎ 0 2635 8800
🚈 Skytrain Silom and Chong Nonsi

MANHATTAN

www.hotelmanhattan.com
This modern, good-value hotel is in a central location just off Sukhumvit, and has 203 spacious and tastefully decorated rooms. The service here is friendly, and there is a good bar and equally good restaurant.
🕂 G6 ✉ 13 Soi Sukhumvit 15 ☎ 0 2255 0166 🚈 Skytrain Asoke
🚇 Sukhumvit

ME STYLE PLACE

www.mestyleplace.com
Step into the colorful
lobby here, very retro in
style with old scooters
and a roofless mini as a
reception desk. The funky
approach to decor con-
tinues into the 89 rooms,
some with balconies.
🔲 J3 ✉ 22–20 Mituna Soi
13, Huay Kwang ☎ 0 2690
5884 🚇 Huay Kwang

MUSE

www.hotelmusebangkok.com
This modern and stylish
hotel is situated on the
relatively quiet Langsuan
Road, just a short walk
from the Skytrain. Even
the standard rooms here
push the boundaries
in comfort and lovely
furnishings while the
19th-floor infinity pool
and rooftop bar all add to
the appeal.
🔲 F6 ✉ 55/555 Langsuan
Road, Lumphini, Pathumwan
☎ 0 2630 4000 🚇 Skytrain
Chit Lom

OLD BANGKOK INN

www.oldbangkokinn.com
This picturesque old shop
house, converted into a
stylish boutique hotel,
offers small rooms in
colors reflecting the floral
names of each room.
🔲 C5 ✉ 609 Thanon
Phra Sumen ☎ 0 2629
1787 🚤 Khlong taxi to Tha
Phan Fah

LA RÉSIDENCE

www.laresidencebangkok.com
This is a small boutique
hotel located above the
All Gaengs restaurant
(curries are their spe-
cialty) on Surawong. La
Résidence has 26 lovely
rooms with cable TV, air-
conditioning and minibar.
🔲 E7 ✉ 173/8–9 Thanon
Surawong ☎ 0 2233 3301
🚇 Skytrain Chong Nonsi

THE SIAM HERITAGE

www.thesiamheritage.com
Close to both the Skytrain
and the Metro, this
charming boutique hotel
is in an excellent
location. The 73 rooms
and suites reflect tra-
ditional Thai style with
polished wooden floors
and antique teak furniture
complemented by Thai
silk accents. Amenities
include a Thai restaurant,
rooftop swimming pool
and spa.
🔲 E7 ✉ 115/1 Surawong
Road, Bangrak ☎ 0 2353

A RANGE OF HOTELS

In the top end and budget
category of accommoda-
tions you more or less get
the hotel you pay for, but
in the mid-range things are
less clear. The lobby usually
looks good but the rooms
may not be of the same
standard. You may also find
that there is a coming and
going of massage girls or
call girls during the night.
The hotels mentioned on
these pages all have some
character, are clean, and
prefer guests to go up to
their room alone.

6101 🚇 Skytrain Sala Daeng
🚇 Samyan

THE SWISS LODGE

www.swisslodge.com
The Swiss Lodge is a
boutique hotel on a quiet
street off Silom Road.
The 55 rooms are
spotless, equipped with
air-conditioning, Internet
and TV. There's a small
pool and sundeck on the
roof terrace.
🔲 E–F7 ✉ 3 Thanon
Convent, Silom 15 ☎ 0 2233
5345 🚇 Skytrain Sala Daeng

THAI HOUSE HOTEL

www.thaihouse.co.th
Experience living in a
traditional Thai house
at this hotel, set in an
orchard 14 miles (22km)
north of Bangkok. Also
here, you can attend an
organized cookery class
and accompanied trip to
the local markets.
🔲 Off map ✉ 32/4 Moo 8,
Tambol Bangmaung, Amphoe
Bangyai, Nonthaburi ☎ 0
2903 9354 🚤 From Tha
Chang, public ferry to Bang Yai
in Nonthaburi, then water taxi
to Thai House Hotel

VIENGTAI HOTEL

www.viengtai.co.th
This is a typical mid-range
Chinese hotel in the
street parallel to Khao
San, with comfortable
rooms in a modern
building. Not a lot of
charm but good value
and good location.
🔲 C5 ✉ 42 Thanon
Rambuttri, Banglamphu ☎ 0
2280 5434 🚤 Tha Phra Athit

Luxury Hotels

PRICES

Expect to pay over 4,000B per night for a luxury hotel.

BANYAN TREE

www.banyantree.com
One of the tallest hotels in town, with an excellent spa. The view from the rooftop and the 62nd-floor restaurant are stupendous. All 216 rooms are equipped with the latest office gadgets and there's a pool and excellent restaurants.
🕂 F7 ✉ 21/100 South Sathorn Road ☎ 0 2679 1200 🚇 Skytrain Sala Daeng Ⓜ Lumphini

FOUR SEASONS BANGKOK

www.fourseasons.com/bangkok
An impressive modern hotel in the heart of Bangkok with a grand, old-style atmosphere, imposing lobby, shopping arcade and 354 lovely, elegant rooms.
🕂 F6 ✉ 155 Ratchadamri Road ☎ 0 2126 8866 🚇 Skytrain Ratchadamri

LOY LA LANG

www.loylalang.com
For those who prefer small and luxurious rather than large international hotels, this seven-room teak house is a haven right on the Chao Phraya River in the peaceful grounds of Wat Pathumkongka.

Guests find it hard to tear themselves away from the river view terrace to bother with the available TV or WiFi.
🕂 D6 ✉ 1620/2 Songwat Road, Sampanthawong ☎ 0 2639 1390 🚇 Hua Lamphong 🚢 Tha Ratchawongse

MANDARIN ORIENTAL

The Mandarin Oriental is a Bangkok institution (▷ 58). The hotel has sumptuous rooms in the modern building and suites in the older wing.

METROPOLITAN BY COMO

www.comohotels.com/metropolitanbangkok
A trendy, minimalist hotel oozing design. The 169 light-filled rooms have complimentary WiFi and the hotel features an award-winning restaurant, pool, yoga studio and spa.
🕂 F7 ✉ 27 South Sathorn, Tungmahamek Sathorn ☎ 0 2625 3333 Ⓜ Lumphini

ASIAN LUXURY

There is no shortage of luxury hotels in Bangkok, and the standards of their rooms and service are among the best in the world. Check that the room rate includes breakfast (American buffet or continental) as it is usually expensive. In the low season most hotels will also reduce their rates by 25–50 percent when asked.

PENINSULA

www.peninsula.com/bangkok
A wonderful hotel, considered to be one of the best in the world. There are 370 fully equipped rooms, all with excellent views of the river and large, sumptuous marble bathrooms with TVs. The restaurants are excellent, and there is a three-tiered swimming pool in the garden. Superb service.
🕂 D7 ✉ 333 Thanon Chareon Nakorn ☎ 0 2861 2888 🚇 Skytrain Saphan Taksin, then free shuttle boat 🚢 Free shuttle boats from Oriental, River City and Shangri-La piers

SHANGRI-LA

www.shangri-la.com
Elegant 802-room hotel—most rooms overlook the river. It has two pools in gardens with ponds, shrines and a spirit house. The Krungthep Wing offers more luxury and balconies.
🕂 D7 ✉ 89 Soi Wat Suan Plu, off Thanon Charoen Krung ☎ 0 2236 7777 🚇 Skytrain Saphan Taksin 🚢 Tha Shangri-La pier

SUKHOTHAI HOTEL

www.sukhothai.com
Remarkable hotel in the business district, designed in a contemporary Thai minimalist style. The 226 rooms are decorated with granite, teak and silks. Fine restaurants.
🕂 F7 ✉ 13/3 South Sathorn Road ☎ 0 2344 8888 Ⓜ Lumphini

Use this section to help you plan your visit to Bangkok. We have suggested the best ways to get around the city and useful information for when you are there.

Need to Know

Planning Ahead

When to Go

The most pleasant time to visit, and the peak tourist season, is from November to early March, so flights and lodgings are best reserved ahead. During the hot season, invest in an air-conditioned room. In the rainy season, peaking in September to October, it's wettest at dusk. Frequent floods at this time bring traffic to a standstill.

TIME

Bangkok is 12 hours ahead of EST. In winter: UK is 7 hours behind, Europe 6 hours, New York 12 hours, Australia 3 hours. In summer add 1 hour.

AVERAGE DAILY MAXIMUM TEMPERATURES

JAN	FEB	MAR	APR	MAY	JUN	JUL	AUG	SEP	OCT	NOV	DEC
83°F	83°F	85°F	86°F	87°F	87°F	86°F	87°F	87°F	86°F	85°F	83°F
28°C	28°C	29°C	30°C	31°C	31°C	30°C	31°C	31°C	30°C	29°C	28°C

Bangkok has three distinct seasons:

Hot season (March to May)—The climate can be unbearable because the high temperatures are intensified by the 90 percent humidity.

Rainy season (June to October)—Hot and humid days are followed by rain, usually at dusk.

Cool season (November to February)—The sky is usually bright and clear; days are reasonably cool and nights pleasantly warm.

WHAT'S ON

January/February
Chinese New Year: Temples are busy, shops close.
Maga Puja: Candle-lit processions at *wats* for full moon.
March *Kite fights and festivals*: (Mar–Apr): On Sanam Luang.
Chakri Day (6 Apr): Celebrates the founding in 1782 of the Chakri dynasty.
April *Songkran* (mid-Apr): The Thai New Year.
May *Royal Plowing Ceremony* (early May): Start of the rice-planting

season on Sanam Luang.
Visaka Puja (mid-May): Celebrates the birth, enlightenment and death of the Buddha.
July *Asalha Puja*: Marks Buddha's first sermon and the start of a three-month Rains Retreat.
Bangkok International Film Festival: With more than 150 films from around the world.
August *HM Queen Sirikit's Birthday* (12 Aug).
September/October
Moon Festival: The Chinese community honors the moon goddess.

October *Ok Pansa*: End of the three-month Rains Retreat. Monks are presented with new robes and gifts.
November *Loy Krathong* (Nov full moon): Small banana-leaf boats with flowers and candles float in celebration of water spirits. *Long-boat races*.
December *Trooping the Color*: Starts a week of celebrations for the King's birthday (5 Dec).

Bangkok Online

www.tourismthailand.org
Official site of the Tourism Authority of Thailand with a range of information on Thai art, culture and food, as well as practical information, links to official websites and listings.

www.bangkoksite.com
Useful information about Bangkok's main sights with plenty of pictures and information on how to get there and what else to do in the city.

www.bangkokpost.com
Online offering of the daily *Bangkok Post* with news items, economic reviews, weather reports, restaurant reviews and articles on the capital's sights, culture and art.

www.bangkok.com
Comprehensive guide to the city's temples, museums, hotels, markets, great shopping and exotic nightlife, as well as tips to make the most of your stay.

www.thebigchilli.com
Online version of the Bangkok *Big Chilli* magazine with the latest information and listings.

www.into-asia.com
Easy-to-use site that gives a general insight into Thai language and culture. Useful advice about scams and tourist traps.

www.bk.asia-city.com
Insider's guide to Bangkok with what's on and reviews of new and old restaurants, nightlife venues and shops.

www.thailandforvisitors.com
Useful site for planning your visit to the city. It provides information on sights, shopping, accommodations and restaurants and cafés, plus practical tips.

TRAVEL SITE

www.fodors.com
A complete travel-planning site. You can research prices and weather; reserve air tickets, cars and rooms; ask questions (and get answers) from fellow travelers.

INTERNET ACCESS

The days of having to seek out Internet cafés in Bangkok are long gone and the city's hotels, bars, restaurants and other public places are as good as any in offering reliable WiFi connections, more often than not at no charge.

Getting There

VISAS AND TRAVEL INSURANCE

For the latest passport and visa information, go to the United States embassy website at http:/bangkok. usembassy.gov or the British embassy website at www.gov.uk/government/ world/thailand. Check your insurance: It is vital that your travel insurance covers medical expenses, in addition to accidents, trip cancellation, baggage loss and theft. Check the policy covers any continuing treatment for chronic conditions. Keep all receipts in case you need to make a claim.

DON MUEANG AIRPORT

The airport has ATMs, 24-hour booths, currency exchange, car rental and hotel desks, official taxi counters, an official tourist information counter (daily 8am–midnight), left-luggage office, post office, Internet access points and a number of places to eat and drink, some of which are open 24 hours. A covered walkway connects all three terminals. The airport is now used for domestic flights since Suvarnabhumi airport opened. For general information about the airport, tel 02 5351 111.

AIRPORTS

Bangkok's main international airport is Suvarnabhumi (suvarnabhumiairport.com), located 15 miles (25km) east of downtown Bangkok.

ARRIVING BY AIR

Suvarnabhumi airport is served by excellent transportation links to the city and beyond.

● There is a free express bus service connecting the 2nd floor (gate 5) and the 5th floor (gate 5) of the terminal building with the public transportation center.

● Four local bus routes (lines A, B, C and D) operating within the airport connect services, facilities, businesses and offices, including other floors and gates of the passenger terminal, the Novotel Hotel and long-term parking.

● An efficient air rail link operates between Suvarnabhumi and the city center and takes 15–30 minutes. The service connects with the Phaya Thai BTS Skytrain station (which does have a lot of stairs) and the terminal Makkasan station. A single ticket is 90B, return 150B.

● Airports of Thailand Limited operates 24-hour limousines (tel 2134 2323/5). The service counter is on the second floor at baggage claim and arrival hall exits, channels A, B and C. Prices vary but expect to pay around 1,500B for a transfer from the airport to the city.

● Taxis operate from the 1st floor of the passenger terminal (gates 4 and 7). The service is 24 hours. There are (usually)

manned terminals where you collect a ticket showing the number of the lane opposite at which your taxi will pull up. Taxis are metered and prices vary but expect to pay 300B for a journey to the Sukhumvit area. Note that there are two tolls on the main route into the city (one is 25B, the second 50B). Your driver may expect you to pay this rather than add it to your fare so be sure to have some smaller notes on you. Note: do not use taxis from other sources as these are invariably operated by touts.

● If you have a connecting flight out of Don Muaeng airport there is a transfer bus operating between 5am and midnight. It departs from the 2nd floor (gate 3) of the terminal building (if you're arriving from Don Muaeng it will drop you on the 4th floor at gate 5). In both directions the service operates hourly between 5am and 10am and from 10pm to midnight and more frequently from 10am to 10pm.

● There are several bus routes from the public transportation center to various parts of Bangkok, however we don't recommend these—see Getting Around ▷ 118–119.

ARRIVING BY TRAIN

Trains from and to Malaysia and Singapore use Hua Lamphong Station, which connects with the MRT subway system which, in turn, connects with the BTS Skytrain (two stops from Hua Lamphong and use the nearby Sala Daeng Skytrain station). Or, take a taxi but make sure it's metered or agree a fixed fare.

CUSTOMS

Licenses are required to export antiques, art objects and religious articles (▷ 62, panel). No more than 50,000B may be exported. Those with valid tourist visas may apply for a VAT refund (7 percent) on purchases from certain shops and stores. Papers need to be filled in at the stores. At Departures in the airport you fill in an application with the goods and receipts for the refund.

VACCINATIONS

Check with your doctor which vaccinations are recommended. Proof of vaccination against yellow fever will be demanded when coming from an infected country.

Getting Around

BTS SKYTRAIN

The elevated BTS Skytrain (tel 0 2617 7300, www.bts.co.th) is by far the fastest, coolest and most comfortable way to get around. Trains run every few minutes from 6am to midnight at 15–42B a trip. There are two lines, Silom and Sukhumvit, and neither serves the old city. The only change between lines is at Siam Station. The Metro (Bangkok Metro Public Company, tel 0 2624 5200, www.bangkokmetro.co.th) operates the 12-mile (20km) Blue Line from Hua Lamphong Station to Bang Sue. There are 18 stations including three that link up with the Skytrain. Both Bangkok's subway and Skytrain have extensions either under construction or at the planning stage. Fares are 16–42B; a day pass costs 120B.

The best way to see the old city is to take the Skytrain to Saphan Taksin and connect with the Chao Phraya River Express Boats (www.chaophrayaexpressboat.co.th), which serve piers (*tha*; marked on the fold-out map). They avoid traffic and are fast, enjoyable and inexpensive (10–40B; a one-day pass costs 150B). Boats run about every 10 minutes daily 6–6 or 7. It's also possible to hire a long-tail boat for a personalized tour of the city's *klongs* or to a destination of your choice. Prices vary. Ask your hotel concierge or tour operator/guide for advice.

BOATS

Boats not flying any flag will stop at piers where people are waiting to board or passengers are waiting to disembark. Boats flying a yellow or orange flag are express boats that do not stop at every pier. A dark blue flag shows that this is the last one of the day. Special Tourist Boats run between Central Pier and Banglamphu, and the ticket allows you to hop on and off any of these boats.

BUSES

Although there is an extensive bus network, it is not advisable to use them. Aside from it being very difficult to access accurate information on

numbers and routes (most information is in Thai), buses are overcrowded, hot and sticky, and can be a haunt of pickpockets. And with the superb BTS Skytrain and MRT Metro (or the good, old-fashioned *tuk-tuk*) the many alternatives are clean, efficient and safe.

TAXIS

These are usually air-conditioned and metered —check it is switched on. The flag fare is 35B. A 24-hour phone-a-cab service charges 20B over the metered fare (Siam Taxi, tel 1161 and Taxi Radion, tel 1681). It is better to arrange through your hotel or guest house. Motorcycle taxis are cheaper and faster, but can be dangerous.

Tuk-tuks

Tuk-tuks can be found everywhere in Bangkok and sometimes are useful for short trips if you're in a rush. A ride in an exotic three-wheel *tuk-tuk* "taxi," even the rare one driven in a calm manner, will expose you to traffic fumes and noise to an alarming degree. Two people, three at the very most, can sit comfortably. Having coins helps when paying the fare, which should always be agreed beforehand. Expect to pay from 40B upward for a short journey.

DRIVING

This is definitely not a good idea. In Bangkok the density of traffic and the bewildering mix of traffic directions and lanes—which are subject to constant changes and are not signposted in English—make driving very challenging. Car rental at Bangkok's Suvarnabhumi airport is feasible if you are not heading into the city, and expressways, signposted in English, connect the airports with routes to other parts of the country. A non-Thai driver is supposed to show an international driver's license when renting a vehicle, but in practice it is often sufficient to show your national license. Larger fuel stations will accept payment by recognized international credit cards, but in rural areas cash may be required.

ORGANIZED SIGHTSEEING

Bangkok has many tour operators, and most hotels have a counter that offers excursions.
Counter Pradit Boat (tel 0 2237 0077, ext. 180) runs daily river and canal tours from the River City Shopping Complex pier. ABC Amazing Bangkok Cyclist Tours organizes bicycle tours in Thonburi, Monday to Friday (tel 0 2665 6364, www.realasia. net). The company offers half-day tours as well as an evening option that includes dinner. The Manohra cruise boats, beautifully restored teak rice barges, do sunset river cruises or overnight trips to Ayutthaya (tel 0 2477 0770, www.manohra cruises.com).

TOURIST INFORMATION

Association of Thai Travel Agents
● ✉ Counter at Suvarnabhumi Airport Level 2, Arrivals Hall
🕐 24 hours
Main TAT office
● ✉ 1600 New Petchaburi Road, Makkasan
☎ 0 2250 5500, www.tourismthailand.org
🕐 Mon–Fri 8–5

Essential Facts

NEED TO KNOW ESSENTIAL FACTS

MONEY MATTERS

● Credit cards are widely accepted, although some places may add a surcharge.
● You can withdraw Thai Baht with credit cards from ATMs.

MONEY

The currency is the Baht (B), divided into 100 satang. The coins are 25 and 50 satang, 1 Baht, 5 Baht and 10 Baht. Notes are 10, 20, 50, 100, 500 and 1,000 Baht.

EMBASSIES

US Embassy
✉ 120–122 Thanon Witthaya and 95 Thanon Witthaya
☎ 0 2205 4000, http:/bangkok.usembassy.gov

Canadian Embassy
✉ 15th Floor, Abdulrahim Place, 990 Thanon Rama IV
☎ 0 2646 4300, thailand.gc.ca

British Embassy
✉ 14 Thanon Witthaya, Lumphini Pathumwan
☎ 0 2305 8333, www.gov.uk/government/world/thailand

Spanish Embassy
✉ 93/98–99 Lake Rajada Office, Ratchadapisek Road, Klongtoey
☎ 0 2661 8284

ELECTRICITY

● 220V, 50-cycle AC. Most hotels have 110V shaver outlets.

EMERGENCIES

● Bangkok is generally safe, but watch for pickpockets and bag-snatchers in crowded places, especially buses, boats and ferries. Women should take care alone at night.
● Leave valuables and travel documents in your hotel's safety deposit box (leave copies of travel documents at home). Exercise care when dealing with money and credit cards while out.
● Take care of credit cards. Keep all receipts and destroy carbons.
● Beware of "bargain" gems, jewelry or other objects, which might later prove to be worthless. Also beware of getting involved in a game of Thai cards as you are sure to lose.
● Beware of taking someone to your room, or of accepting food or drink from strangers, as there have been cases of visitors being drugged and robbed.
● Thais are serious about wanting to stop drug smuggling. Border security is efficient and the maximum penalty is death.

MEDICAL TREATMENT

● All listed hospitals have 24-hour emergency services, but you may need your passport and a deposit of 20,000B. Your medical insurance policy may not be accepted, although major credit cards are.
● Private hospitals: BNH Hospital, 9 Thanon Convent, tel 0 2686 2700;
St Louis Hospital, 27 Thanon South Sathorn, tel 0 2210 9999.
● Public hospitals: Bumrungrad Hospital, 33 Soi 3 Sukhumvit, tel 0 2667 1000;
Samitivej Hospital, 133 Soi 49, Thanon Sukhumvit, tel 0 2711 8181.
● Contact your hotel reception first in case of a medical emergency.
● Keep all receipts for claims on your travel insurance when back home.

MEDICINES
● British Dispensary, near Soi 5, 109 Thanon Sukhumvit (tel 0 2252 8056) or at corner of Soi Oriental and Thanon Charoen Krung (New Road, tel 0 2234 0174).
● Foodland Supermarket Pharmacy, 1413 Soi 5 Thanon Sukhumvit (tel 0 2254 2247, open 24 hours).
● Thai pharmacies are generally well stocked, and many drugs are available over the counter.
● Pharmacies are open early morning to mid or late evening. Many pharmacists speak English.

OPENING HOURS
● Offices: Mon–Fri 8.30–noon, 1–4.30.
● Banks: Mon–Fri 10–3.30.
● Bangkok Bank and exchange counters: Daily 7am–8pm (some open to 9pm).
● Shops: Mon–Sun 10–6.30 or 7; smaller shops often stay open 12 hours a day. Most shopping centers are open daily 10am–9pm.

POST OFFICES
● The General Post Office (GPO) is at Thanon Charoen Krung (New Road), between the Oriental and Sheraton hotels (open Mon–Fri 8–8, Sat, Sun and holidays 8–1).
● Stamps cost 30B for airmail letters and 15B for postcards to the US, Europe and Australia.

TELEPHONES
● The Thaicard is an international prepaid phone card available at post offices, bookshops and 7-Eleven stores in values of 100B and 2,000B.
● From 9pm–midnight, 5am–7am there is a 20 percent discount on international calls; from midnight–5am the discount is 30 percent.
● All Thai phone numbers now have eight digits. Even when calling within Bangkok the "0" area code should always be used.
● The least expensive way to call internationally is via the Internet. WiFi is widely available in Thailand and is free in many hotels, bars, restaurants and public places.

EMERGENCY PHONE NUMBERS
● Ambulance ☎ 191
● Fire ☎ 199
● Police ☎ 191
● Tourist Assistance Center ☎ 0 2282 8129

TOURIST POLICE
● If you are a victim of theft, call the tourist police ☎ 1155 or 1699

ETIQUETTE
● Thais show great respect for their royal family and religious personalities, as should visitors.
● Women should not touch monks, who also cannot receive offerings directly from them.
● All Buddha images are sacred.
● A public display of anger is taboo.
● Cover arms and legs in temples.
● It is insulting to touch someone's head or back, and it is rude to point toes or the soles of feet at someone or at a Buddha image. Remove shoes upon entering a temple or a private home.
● Thais rarely shake hands, instead placing them together under their chin in a *wai*.

Language

Although English is widely spoken in hotels and restaurants, it is useful to have some Thai. It is quite difficult to get the hang of, as one syllable can be pronounced in five tones, each of which will carry a different meaning. The classic example of this is the syllable *mai*, which, in the different tones, can mean "new," "wood," "burned," "not?" and "not." So *Mái mài mâi mâi mäi* means: "New wood doesn't burn, does it?" Consonants are also pronounced slightly differently. Ask a local Thai to pronounce the words listed below for you in the right tone. And for taxi and *tuk-tuk* drivers, ask someone to write down your destination in Thai script.

THE BASICS	
hello	*sawat-dii krap (man)*, *sawat-dii (woman)*
how are you?	*pen yangai?*
I'm fine	*sabaay dii*
thank you	*khawp khun*
good morning	*sawatdee*
good afternoon/ good evening	*sawadee*
good-bye	*laa gorn*
see you later	*phop gan mai*
sorry, excuse me	*kor toh*
what is your name?	*khun cheu arai?*
my name is…(man)	*phom cheu*
my name is… (woman)	*diichan cheu*
Do you speak English?	*Khun poot pah-sah angkrit dai mai?*
(I) don't understand	*mai khao jai*
yes	*chai*
no	*mai chai*
how do I get to…?	*pai…yng ngai?*
turn right	*lii-o kwaa*
turn left	*lii-o sai*
straight ahead	*dtrong dtrong*
how much?	*thao rai?*
inexpensive	*thuuk*
too expensive	*phaeng pai*
here	*tee-nee*
where	*tee-n*
there	*tee-nan*
when	*muae-rai*

NUMBERS	
0	*suun*
1	*neung*
2	*sawng*
3	*sahm*
4	*sii*
5	*haa*
6	*hok*
7	*jet*
8	*paet*
9	*kao*
10	*sip*
11	*sip-et*
12	*sip-sawng*
20	*yii-sip*
30	*sahm-sip*
100	*neeung roy*

GETTING AROUND

on/to the right	yoo/bpai taang kwah
on/to the left	yoo/bpai taang saai
opposite	dtrong-kaam
straight on	dtrong bpai
north	nuae
south	dtai
east	dta-wan-ork
west	ta-wan-tok

DAYS/TIME

Monday	wan jan
Tuesday	wan ang-karn
Wednesday	wan put
Thursday	wanpa-ru-hat-sa-bordee
Friday	wan suk
Saturday	wan sau
Sunday	wan ah-tit
day	glang-wan
today	wan-nee
yesterday	muae-waan-nee
tomorrow	wan-prung-nee

USEFUL WORDS

toilet	hawng suam
river	mae, maee nam lak nam
restaurant	raan aahaa
long-tail boat	ruea hang yao
river bank	rim nam
hotel	rohng raem
train	rot fai
bus	rot meh, rot bat
taxi	rot yon
airport	sanaam
station	sathaanii
main chapel of a temple	bot
pagoda	chedi
foreigner	farang

MORE USEFUL WORDS

open	bpert
closed	bpit
entrance	taang kao
exit	taang org
canal	khlong
alley	soi
bridge	sa-paan
black	see dam
white	see kaow
bicycle	rot jak-gra-yarn
help	chuoy duoy
embassy	sa-taan-toot
temple	wat

MONTHS

January	mak-ga-rah-kom
February	gum-pah-pan
March	mee-nah-kom
April	may-sah-yon
May	pruet-sa-pah-kom
June	mi-tu-nah-yon
July	ga-rak-ga-dah-kom
August	sing-hah/kom
September	gan-yah-yon
October	dtu-lah-kom
November	pruet-sa-ji-gah-yon
December	tan-wah-kom

Timeline

POLITICAL THAILAND

Thailand has had a somewhat turbulent political and democratic track record. Military coups have been common, governments have come and gone with lightning speed, and the military—long an influential and powerful backbone of Thai society—have often "stepped-in" when necessary. Occasional incidents of civil unrest and disruption do happen but they have traditionally been contained to small areas of Bangkok. Before you travel, check the latest travel advice with the State Department in the United States (www.state.gov/travel) or the Foreign and Commonwealth Office in the UK (www.gov.uk/foreign-travel-advice).

From left: King Chulalongkorn (Rama V) in European dress; portrait of King Chulalongkorn (Rama V); portrait of King Bhumibol Adulyadej, in a decorative frame backed by the national colors and displayed during his birthday celebrations

1530s King Phrajai (ruled 1534–46) re-routes the Chao Phraya River creating Thonburi on the west bank and Bang Makok on the east.

1825 King Rama III (ruled 1824–51) closes the mouth of the Chao Phraya River to impose isolationist policies and to resist change.

1851 King Rama IV (ruled 1851–68) encourages change and Thailand retains independence during the colonial period.

1868 Rama V (King Chulalongkorn, ruled 1868–1910) continues social reforms.

1932 A bloodless coup replaces absolute monarchy with a constitutional monarchy. King Prajadhipok (Rama VII, ruled 1925–35) abdicates in 1935.

1939 The country's name is changed from Siam to Prathet Thai.

1946 Thailand is admitted to the United Nations. King Bhumibol Adulyadej (King Rama IX) becomes (and still is) ruling monarch.

2004 On 26th December the Indian Ocean tsunami claims more than 5,000 lives along Thailand's Andaman Coast.

2007 General election is won by the PPP (People Power Party).

2008 Samak Sundaravej is sworn in as prime minister. Protesters demand Samak and his government step down.

2009 Mass rallies take place against the government's economic policies.

2011 The pro-Thaksin Pheu Thai party wins a landslide election victory. Yingluck Shinawatra becomes prime minister.

2012 Anti-government protesters blockade parliament, fearing a proposed amnesty would enable the return of Thaksin Shinawatra. Police demonstrate in Bangkok and call for the over-throw of prime minister Yingluck Shinawatra.

2013 In response to opposition pressure, Yingluck Shinawatra announces early elections will be held in February 2014.

2014 In February, general elections go ahead but the Constitutional Court declares them invalid. In May, the court orders Prime Minister Yingluck Shinawatra and several ministers out of office. The army seizes power in an August coup and General Prayuth Chan-ocha is made prime minister. In November, finance minister Sommai Phasee says new elections are unlikely until 2016.

2015 On April 2nd, King Bhumibol Adulyadej gives his approval for the lifting of martial law in Thailand.

WEST MEETS EAST

In the 1960s, the US began building military bases within Thailand to help with the Vietnam War. The needs of the US military brought huge sums of money into Thailand and helped transform Bangkok into the burgeoning modern city it is today.

From left: A traffic police-man wearing a mask; the bronze statue of King Rama VI in Bangkok, in full military uniform; a portrait of King Bhumibol Adulyadej (King Rama IX)

Index

Published by AA Publishing, a trading name of AA Media Limited, whose registered office is Fanum House, Basing View, Basingstoke, Hampshire RG21 4EA. Registered number 06112600.

© **AA Media Limited 2016**
First published 1997
New edition 2016

WRITTEN BY Anthony Sattin and Sylvie Franquet
UPDATED By David Leck and Anita Sach
SERIES EDITOR Clare Ashton
DESIGN WORK Tracey Freestone
IMAGE RETOUCHING AND REPRO Ian Little

Colour separation by AA Digital Department
Printed and bound by Leo Paper Products, China

A CIP catalogue record for this book is available from the British Library.

ISBN 978-0-7495-7737-7

A05378
Maps in this title produced from map data supplied by Global Mapping, Brackley, UK. Copyright © Global Mapping and data from openstreetmap.org © OpenStreetMap contributors
Transport map © Communicarta Ltd, UK

The Automobile Association wishes to thank the following photographers, companies and picture libraries for their assistance in the preparation of this book.

2/3t AA/J Holmes; 4/5t AA/J Holmes; 4 AA/D Henley; 5 AA/J Holmes; 6/7t AA/J Holmes; 6cl AA/R Strange; 6cc AA/D Henley; 6cr AA/D Henley; 6bl A/R Strange; 6bc AA/D Henley; 6br AA/J Holmes; 7cl AA/J Holmes; 7cc AA/J Holmes; 7cr AA/D Henley; 7bl AA/J Holmes; 7br AA/J Holmes; 8/9t AA/J Holmes; 10/11t AA/J Holmes; 10tr AA/J Holmes; 10ctr AA/J Holmes; 10/1c AA/J Holmes; 10/1b AA/J Holmes; 11tl AA/J Holmes; 11tc AA/J Holmes; 12/3t AA/J Holmes; 13tl AA/J Holmes; 13ctl AA/J Holmes; 13c AA/J Holmes; 13bl AA/J Holmes; 14/5t J AA/J Holmes; 14tr AA/J Holmes; 14ctr AA/D Henley; 14bcr AA/J Holmes; 14br AA/J Holmes; 15 AA/J Holmes; 16/17t AA/J Holmes; 16t J AA/J Holmes; 16tc AA/J Holmes; 16bc AA/D Henley; 16b AA/J Holmes; 17t A/R Strange; 17tc A/R Strange; 17bc A/R Strange; 17b AA/J Holmes; 18t AA/J Holmes; 18tc AA/J Holmes; 18c AA/D Henley; 18cb AA/J Holmes; 18b AA/J Holmes; 19(i) A/R Strange; 19(ii) J AA/J Holmes; 19(iii) AA/D Henley; 19(iv) A/R Strange; 20/1 A/R Strange; 24l AA/D Henley; 24/5t AA/D Henley; 24/5b AA/D Henley; 25tr AA/D Henley; 25bl AA/D Henley; 25br AA/D Henley; 26l AA/J Holmes; 26r AA/J Holmes; 27l AA/J Holmes; 27r J AA/J Holmes; 28l AA/D Henley; 28/9 AA/D Henley; 30l A/R Strange; 30r A/R Strange; 31 A/R Strange; 32 A/R Strange; 32/3 A/R Strange; 33 A/R Strange; 34l A/R Strange; 34/5t A/R Strange; 34/5b AA/D Henley; 35t AA/J Holmes; 35bl AA/D Henley; 35br AA/D Henley; 36l A/R Strange; 36/7t A/R Strange; 36/7b AA/D Henley; 37t A/R Strange; 37bl A/R Strange; 37bc A/R Strange; 37br A/R Strange; 38 AA/J Holmes; 38/9 AA/J Holmes; 40l AA/J Holmes; 40c AA/J Holmes; 40r AA/J Holmes; 41l AA/J Holmes; 41r A/R Strange; 42/3t AA/J Holmes; 42bl Nunnicha Supagrit / Alamy; 42br A/R Strange; 43b A/R Strange; 44 AA/J Holmes; 45 AA/J Holmes; 46 AA/J Holmes; 47 AA/J Holmes; 48 AA/J Holmes; 49 AA/J Holmes; 52l AA/J Holmes; 52/3t AA/J Holmes; 52/3b AA/J Holmes; 53t AA/J Holmes; 53bl AA/J Holmes; 53br AA/J Holmes; 54l AA/J Holmes; 54/5t AA/J Holmes; 54br AA/J Holmes; 55bl AA/J Holmes; 55r AA/J Holmes; 56l AA/J Holmes; 56r AA/J Holmes; 57l A/R Strange; 57c A/R Strange; 57r AA/J Holmes; 58/9t AA/J Holmes; 58bl AA/J Holmes; 58br A/R Strange; 59b AA/J Holmes; 60 AA/J Holmes; 61 AA/J Holmes ; 62 AA/J Holmes; 63 AA/J Holmes; 64 AA/J Holmes; 65 AA/J Holmes; 66 AA/J Holmes ; 67 AA/J Holmes; 68 AA/J Holmes; 69 AA/J Holmes; 72 AA/J Holmes; 73tl AA/J Holmes; 73tc AA/J Holmes; 73tr AA/J Holmes; 74l AA/D Henley; 74tr AA/D Henley; 74br AA/D Henley ; 75t AA/D Henley ; 75bl AA/D Henley; 75br AA/D Henley; 76tl A/R Strange; 76tr AA/J Holmes; 77tr AA/J Holmes; 77tl AA/D Henley; 77tc AA/J Holmes; 78-79 travelbild.com / Alamy; 79 AA/D Henley ; 80 AA/J Holmes; 81tl AA/J Holmes; 81tc AA/J Holmes; 81tr AA/J Holmes; 82/3t AA/J Holmes; 82bl AA/D Henley ; 82br AA/J Holmes; 83bl Eddie Gerald / Alamy; 83br AA/J Holmes; 84t AA/J Holmes; 84b AA/J Holmes; 85 AA/J Holmes; 86 AA/J Holmes; 87 AA/J Holmes; 88 AA/J Holmes; 89 AA/J Holmes; 90 AA/J Holmes; 91 AA/J Holmes; 92 AA/J Holmes; 93 AA/J Holmes; 94 AA/J Holmes; 95 A/R Strange; 98l AA/D Henley; 98/9t AA/D Henley; 98/9b AA/D Henley; 99t AA/D Henley; 99bl AA/D Henley; 99br AA/D Henley; 100tl AA/J Holmes; 100bl AA/J Holmes; 100/1t AA/J Holmes; 100/1b AA/J Holmes; 101t AA/J Holmes; 101bl AA/J Holmes; 101br AA/J Holmes; 102l Prasart Museum; 102c Prasart Museum; 102r Prasart Museum; 103t AA/J Holmes; 103bl dave stamboulis / Alamy; 103br AA/D Henley; 104/5t A/R Strange; 104bl AA/D Henley; 104bc AA/D Henley; 104br A/R Strange ; 105bl A/R Strange; 105blc A/R Strange; 105bcr AA/D Henley; 105br A/R Strange; 106t A/R Strange; 106bl AA/D Henley; 106bcl AA/D Henley; 106bc AA/D Henley; 106bcr AA/D Henley; 106br AA/D Henley; 107 AA/J Holmes; 108/9t AA/C Sawyer ; 108tr AA/D Henley; 108tcr AA/J Holmes; 108bcr AA/J Holmes; 108br AA/J Holmes; 110/1 AA/C Sawyer; 112 AA/C Sawyer; 113 AA/D Henley; 114/5 AA/J Holmes; 116/7t AA/J Holmes; 117b AA/J Holmes; 118/9t AA/J Holmes; 120/1t AA/J Holmes; 122/3t AA/J Holmes; 122b AA/J Holmes; 124/5t AA/J Holmes; 124bl AA/D Henley; 124br AA/D Henley; 124/5b A/R Strange; 125bl A/R Strange; 125bc A/R Strange; 125br AA/D Henley.

Titles in the Series